The Decoding Solution

Rime Magic & Fast Success for Struggling Readers

Sharon Zinke

SCHOLASTIC

New York • Toronto • London • Auckland • Sydney
Mexico City • New Delhi • Hong Kong • Buenos Aires

Dedication

This book is dedicated to all of the children, teens, and adults who have struggled with the printed word. May all children learn to read with ease and with dignity!

Acknowledgments

First I thank my students, all of you, for inspiring me with your magnificence, your willingness to take on a challenge, your unflagging trust in the process, and the stand you take for your own success. Thank you for teaching me what I needed to know in order to make a breakthrough in reading intervention. It was because of you that I was able to write this book.

A special thank you to my editor, Lois Bridges, for trusting and believing in me from the very start. I thank my family and my friends for your love and encouragement and support, for knowing the importance of this endeavor and reminding me that I could make this difference. It was because of you that I was able to write this book.

And the teachers! I thank all of you for your compassion and your dedication, for your determination to serve the students in your classrooms so that they can all shine, for your unwillingness to compromise what you know is best for your students, for knowing your students and always listening for effective ways to meet their individual needs. Thank you for going out of your way to support me in this effort, for constantly reminding me of the magic that happens in classrooms. It was because of you that I was able to write this book.

And finally, I am grateful to all of the teachers and parents who gift me with your trust and give these strategies a try with students who struggle to make sense of print. My heart is with you as you work with your wonderful students. I celebrate your success!

Cover Designer: Brian LaRossa
Editor: Lois Bridges
Copy/Production Editor: Danny Miller
Interior Designer: Sarah Morrow

Printed in the U.S.A.
ISBN: 978-0-545-38263-2

1 2 3 4 5 6 7 8 9 10 40 19 18 17 16 15 14 13

Table of Contents

DVD Contents

A Message from the Author

As I was working out Rime Magic and other strategies with my struggling middle-school students, I had no idea at first that what we created would be so powerful in solving the decoding issues in reading intervention. Almost right away, my sixth-grade RSP students were telling me that reading was "so much easier," even in their grade-level texts. That first year, we saw between two and five years' growth in word-recognition grade-equivalent scores, even though we had so little time in our middle-school special education program to zero in on reading strategies. At that point, I knew that we were on to something that would make a life-changing difference for students who had fallen behind in reading.

After retiring from public school teaching, I have had the chance to bring these strategies to many schools around the San Francisco Bay Area. We are seeing spectacular results when students are able to receive consistent intervention in small groups. Slipping these strategies into the language arts curriculum in elementary school classrooms, we are able to prevent a high percentage of students from falling behind.

If you are a first- or second-grade teacher, you can spend five or ten minutes a day enjoying Rime Magic lessons with your students. This will go a long way toward preventing the decoding problems many students carry with them into middle school. If you teach third through twelfth grades, you can use the strategies in this book to quickly bring your students with low word recognition up to grade level in their decoding skills. Upper-grade students often need very few lessons to make the progress they need. If you are a literacy coach or reading intervention teacher, or if you work with students with special needs, you will find your struggling decoders making quick progress.

There are students in nearly every classroom who are unable to fully participate with their classmates in developing strategies for deep, satisfying reading because they have difficulty with decoding. I am excited to see so many struggling readers break through the decoding barrier and suddenly find themselves able to enjoy a good book.

—*Sharon Zinke*

In every class we teach, we encounter kids, who, for a variety of reasons, fall behind their peers in word recognition. So it's not a stretch to imagine this scenario: testing season is on the horizon and three of your fifth-grade boys are still playing catch-up—you have very little time to get them ready for middle school.

You have tried everything you can think of to try, but these students are still struggling with material at second- and third-grade levels. Their writing and spelling skills are lagging far behind. And yet, these boys are smart and reasonably articulate, and you suspect that if they could just decode more easily they might comprehend and have access to grade-level text.

What if:

- there were a simple set of instructional strategies that you could use to get them caught up in decoding in a matter of weeks even though they are so far behind?
- you could easily get their word recognition up several grade levels in a way that is painless and even fun for them?
- these strategies were so effective that your students, seeing their own fast progress, begged for more?

The Decoding Solution: Rime Magic & Fast Success for Struggling Readers offers easy answers to a difficult question: How do we, in elementary schools, get our struggling decoders caught up with their peers before sending them on to middle and high school where they can easily get lost in their content-area classes and even drop out of school?

Like many of our more-effective approaches to phonics instruction, Rime Magic is based on onset/rime. Because we are learning that separating words between onset and rime is easier for beginning readers (Goswami & Bryant, 1990; Moustafa, 1997), most of the recent phonics or decoding programs include onset/rime activities with one-syllable words. Students are taught common rimes and ways to blend the beginning of the word with the rime. But Rime Magic (explained in detail in Section 2) has a special twist that propels students forward and holds their interest more effectively. Teachers are excited about it because it works and because their students, feeling validated and sensing success, keep asking for more.

Give it a try with a couple of your students who are lagging behind. You'll find that by using Rime Magic, you will make the difference you have wanted to make with students who struggle with print.

What is an onset? A rime?

An onset is the consonant or consonant blend at the beginning of a word that precedes the first vowel. It can be one, two, or three letters long.

- In the word *cat*, the onset is *c*.
- In the word *flat*, the onset is *fl*.
- In the word *splat*, the onset is *spl*.

A rime begins with the first vowel and continues to the end of the syllable. Therefore, in each of the words above, the rime is *at*.

Each syllable has an onset and a rime or just a rime.

CHAPTER 1

Decoding in Its Proper Perspective

Since this book focuses so specifically on decoding, it's important that we place it in its proper perspective. When I read my newspaper in the morning, I am searching for personal meaning. I tend to avoid the articles that add nothing positive to my day and stop to read when I see something about glassblowing or an editorial about education. When I read, my eyes move easily over the words and hesitate for a moment when something doesn't make sense, breaking the flow only until I can again make sense of the print on the page. I'm thinking as I read, questioning, wondering, inferring, seeing pictures in my head, and responding with opinions and sometimes with sadness or a smile.

In my world, reading is all about constructing meaning. I look briefly at most of the letters on the page, but only enough to support the understanding I'm constructing from my own prior knowledge of the subject and my use of syntax, to make sense of the words and ideas. My solid grasp of letter-sound correspondence is a huge support, but decoding is not reading. Not by itself. Decoding is only one of the cueing systems that I use to construct meaning as I read.

When a young child begins to read, he begins by constructing meaning. He reads the pictures. My son Daniel read books every day when he was two and three years old. He sat on the carpet or the couch, turning the pages of his book, telling exciting stories about trucks and dinosaurs and people. When it finally occurred to him that much more of the story could be found in the words on the page, he began to match the letters with their sounds and learn more about the grapho-phonemic cueing system. But his reading started with meaning. I was glad when his kindergarten and first-grade teachers allowed and encouraged their students to focus on meaning first. Comprehension was the goal and meaning was preserved when letters and sounds were presented in the context of a fun story or poem.

Rime Magic is an approach to decoding (and encoding) that allows students to build a solid foundation in phonics in a very short time. In the past few years, with the influx of so many commercial reading programs requiring hours upon hours of phonics instruction in the early grades, our students are being robbed of most of the project-based literacy experiences, valuable discussions, and wide independent reading that veteran reading teachers know should be the core of the reading program in elementary schools. Morning after morning of phonics instruction has, in effect, taken the place of activities that foster reading comprehension and practice in problem solving and ownership of the reading process for our students. Rime Magic brings so much awareness of word structure in such a short time that teachers can focus on metacognition and monitoring of comprehension, questioning, visualizing, inference, and all the other effective comprehension strategies that will send their students into the upper grades as engaged and active readers.

Rime Magic is an approach to decoding (and encoding) that allows students to build a solid foundation in phonics in a very short time.

CHAPTER 2

Who Needs What? Let's Simplify Assessment for Intervention!

In the San Francisco Bay Area, school districts are using a wide variety of assessment methods to find out who needs remediation and how to group students for instruction. In some school districts, reading assessment is comprehensive and guides the instruction so that students participate in literacy activities that meet their needs and deepen their reading proficiency. In the Berkeley Unified School District, for example, teachers use the Teachers College Reading and Writing Project Assessment to determine the strengths and needs of students so that they are able to provide appropriate instructional support and intervention as students enjoy books and strategy discussions each morning in a Readers' Workshop. Other districts use other types of informal reading inventories, such as the Qualitative Reading Inventory, fifth edition (QRI 5), or the Developmental Reading Assessment (DRA), to complete a comprehensive assessment that includes an analysis of miscues and a retelling or at least a set of questions to determine each student's level of comprehension. These assessments are given to individual students who are struggling with reading or, in some school districts, to all students on a regular basis. Teachers acquire the information they need to make appropriate instructional decisions.

On the other hand, in some school districts, teachers do not administer a full assessment that includes a strong emphasis on comprehension. Some of these districts find themselves spending large amounts of money and time assessing students' decoding and fluency, often forgoing the comprehension segment. All too often, students are regularly assessed for fluency with the use of a stopwatch, reinforcing the speed of the reading rather than the problem solving and use of context that are so important to comprehension. Some schools hire extra personnel to test each student individually on a battery of skills, and others hire substitute teachers so that classroom teachers can assess other teachers' students, only to find later that the test results have contributed very little to language arts program decisions or to the ultimate success of the students.

When I go into schools to work with intervention teams (if they are lucky enough to have them) and to help teachers set up structures for effective reading intervention, I have found that discovering what struggling readers need can be a simple process that takes very little time. When students are identified as low-performing readers by teacher observation, by the results of state and district assessments, or through a combination of teacher-created assessment and anecdotal evidence, it is helpful, first of all, to determine whether the problem is related to decoding and word accuracy, to comprehension, or both.

When I begin an assessment in an elementary school to determine the needs of the school's most-struggling readers, the leadership team usually gives me state test results first. In California, we begin with the students who scored Far Below Basic (FBB) or Below Basic (BB) the previous spring. In addition, of course, teachers give their input and provide a list of students who are struggling in their literacy skills.

A Quick Screening

My quick-screening tool is a word-recognition test, made up of a simple set of word lists, to get a word-recognition grade equivalent for each targeted student. Each test takes less than five minutes. Although word-recognition tests are often included as a part of an Informal Reading Inventory such as the Qualitative Reading Inventory 4 (QRI 4), the one that I have found most valid and reliable is the Slosson Oral Reading Test (SORT). I have used this assessment for many years and find that it is both fast and easy to administer. It is a perfect screening tool to see who needs decoding intervention and who does not.

It is important to remember that a word-recognition level is NOT a reading level because comprehension is not being assessed at all. It is a word-recognition grade equivalent. Upper-grade students who score below 3.0 in word recognition receive immediate intervention in Rime Magic. Many of these students do not have a problem with reading comprehension, but have been held back by their difficulty with the fluent recognition of words as they attempt to read grade-level material. The Rime Magic sequence will cause a significant rise in word-recognition levels in a very short period of time, often in just a few lessons!

In a fifth-grade classroom, for example, Jason scores Far Below Basic on his state assessment (CST). When I give him the word-recognition test, he scores 2.1 (grade equivalent), although a strong word-recognition score for his grade level would be 5.0 or higher. This 2.1 score indicates that he needs effective and efficient decoding intervention (Rime Magic) in order to get his word-recognition score above 3.0. At that point, he needs to gain multisyllabic word proficiency. Concurrent with this reading intervention, Jason will benefit from extensive reading of high-interest books at his independent level to build fluency and from participating in the comprehension-based instructional activities taking place in his fifth-grade classroom.

Mariah, on the other hand, while also scoring Far Below Basic on her state assessment the previous spring, scores 6.2 on the word-recognition test. Right away I know that Mariah has no trouble with decoding or word recognition, but is likely having great difficulty with vocabulary, comprehension, or both. She is obviously not a candidate for decoding intervention. After a simple, quick word-recognition test, I know that she (if the state assessment results do indeed reflect to some degree her reading ability) needs reading intervention focusing on comprehension and vocabulary, in addition to plenty of time reading books of interest to her. It is also critically important that Mariah's teacher immediately stop giving her timed fluency tests in which she is asked to read as fast as she can. She needs to slow down and concentrate on meaning, problem solving as she reads, rereading when something doesn't make sense. If fluency tests are continued, then the stopwatch must be downplayed and the student asked to provide a retelling after the reading is complete.

Does this sound too simple? Relax and rejoice, because a simple word-recognition test is all it takes to get started!

Word-Recognition Grade Equivalent Instructional Response for Struggling Decoders

.1 to 3.0	Lots of Independent, Guided, Shared Reading and RIME MAGIC
3.0 to 3.5	Lots of Independent, Guided, Shared Reading; Review RIME MAGIC and Multisyllabic Words (SMILES)
3.5 to 4.0	Lots of Reading and Multisyllabic Words (SMILES)
4.0 and up	LOTS OF READING!

The Teaching/Assessment Loop

In my experience, monitoring progress in the area of decoding and fluency does not require systematic stopwatch-monitored assessments of reading rate. In fact, this type of regular fluency assessment reinforces to children that reading is about speed and has little to do with comprehension, in addition to consistently robbing students of important instructional time. Reading fast is not synonymous with reading well. Instead, if we want to promote fluency and accurate word recognition, I suggest that we flood our classrooms with fascinating books and other reading materials and have students keep a record of books read (see Chapter 13). You can give students who are reading below grade level a Running Record or Miscue Analysis with retelling to determine a reading level, and give another word recognition assessment later in the year to check progress.

For students receiving reading intervention, give a quick word recognition assessment at the beginning of the school year and again as mileposts are met along the way. For example, a fifth grader who begins the year at 2.1 would receive, along with shared, guided, and independent reading, Rime Magic lessons until he has developed proficiency with the rimes within two- and three-syllable words as he reads independently. At that point, he can be assessed again. Most students will have a score above 3.0 after a few weeks or even days of Rime Magic intervention. Now you can focus on multisyllabic word and spelling strategies to bring his word recognition up to grade level. If multisyllabic word lessons (see Chapter 5) have been woven into content area lessons on a consistent basis in his regular classroom, his word-recognition score may be as high as 3.5 or 4.0, even after just a few weeks. At this point, self-selected independent reading will do the trick, bringing his word recognition to grade level or higher by the end of the year. He will be able to fully participate in the ongoing vocabulary and comprehension instruction and activities that the rest of the class enjoys, without having to struggle to figure out every other word on the page.

CHAPTER 3

Onset/Rime Makes It Easy

How many ways are there to teach phonics? Educators have been studying and arguing about this issue for hundreds of years! In many schools, kindergarten teachers are required to have their young children practice blending and segmenting, breaking words into separate phonemes, a task that is difficult for many students. This practice is based on the dual assumption that phonemic awareness must precede further reading instruction and that blending and segmenting phonemes is necessary in developing phonemic awareness.

However, even some adults who are fluent readers have trouble segmenting words by their individual phonemes and hearing each one as a separate unit. To ask a five-year-old child to respond to the word *stand* by attempting to pronounce each phoneme separately is to take the most isolated, least accessible approach to the introduction of the sounds of letters within words. Phonemic awareness can easily be developed through daily exposure to nursery rhymes, alphabet books, rhyming songs, and any book, poem, or song that makes words sound fun. After teaching young children for many years as a reading specialist and as a resource specialist, I have seen thousands of children successfully learn to read without having to segment phonemes in their kindergarten classrooms. The children who are not as ready to begin focusing on print in kindergarten are the ones most likely to suffer from endless drill in segmenting and blending phonemes.

A phoneme is the smallest unit of sound in a word. The following words are divided into separate phonemes:

c/a/t **d/o/g** **s/m/i/l** **s/t/a/n/d**

The following words are separated between onset and rime:

c at **d og** **sm ile** **st and**

Rather than isolated practice of skills that are written into tests, these youngsters need plenty of authentic literacy experiences, lots of shared reading and writing, and time spent listening to stories read aloud by the teacher or another proficient reader. When young students are introduced to letters and their sounds, it is always best to help them focus on word parts that are easily recognized, and only after exposing them to stories and poems and lists and all manner of exciting, meaningful print. When it's time to look closely at a single word, breaking the word into separate parts based on onset/rime makes sense in the human brain. If I go into a kindergarten or first-grade classroom and play a word game with the class, it might go like this:

Rather than isolated practice of skills that are written into tests, these youngsters need plenty of authentic literacy experiences, lots of shared reading and writing, and time spent listening to stories read aloud by the teacher or another proficient reader.

TEACHER: *I say "cat", you say "at." . . . I say "dog," you say _____.* (Students will right away respond with "og.")

- If I say *smile*, they will respond with "ile."
- If I say *stand*, they will respond with "and."
- If I say *lake*, they will respond with "ake."

Our brains love patterns and want chunks or parcels of letters that we can grab onto and use to make analogies. Between an onset and a rime is an intuitive place to divide words, much easier than dividing words into all of their separate phonemes. In addition, our brain functions as a pattern detector, and we find it much easier to detect patterns than to apply rules (Goswami & Bryant, 1990; Moustafa, 1997).

Teachers like myself who have been teaching in elementary schools for decades have seen phonics techniques and approaches come and go. Some teachers try to keep phonics instruction in the context of meaningful and relevant material. Others teach letter-sound correspondence in a systematic sequence, isolated from connected text. And yet we always seem to have a few students at each grade level who fall far behind in the area of decoding. Because many teachers understand that every child is unique and develops at his or her own pace, struggling readers in their classrooms are no longer referred to as "the low group." They are "emerging readers" or "developing readers," and are given support in their area of need, often in one-on-one conferences or small guided reading groups or in intervention groups within or outside of the classroom if they need an extra boost. When students fall far enough behind their peers, they might work intensively with a reading specialist or are qualified for more-intensive support through special education services. Although these interventions almost always recognize the importance of rimes (in the past referred to as phonograms or word families), there is often a focus on the same isolated phonemic awareness and phonics instruction that did not work for the students in their regular classrooms.

Rime Magic bases instruction on what we have learned from onset/rime research, with an added twist. We begin by teaching rimes, but there is an important difference. Instead of asking students to spend time practicing blending the letters of words such as *mat, sat, cat,* and *flat,* we teach students to recognize the rimes inside two- or three-syllable words. Even high-school students are interested in participating when they quickly find themselves recognizing the *ip* in *sl**ip**pery* or the *at* in *sc**at**tering*, and even the *on* in *resp**on**sibility*!

So . . . let's get started!

CHAPTER 4

Access to the Middle of the Word: The Foundation

It Works Like Magic!

Begin by telling your students that they will be working with Magic Rimes and that these rimes are going to make reading much, much easier. Students who have been in intervention groups for years will want to know that there is something very different going on. They have worked with rimes (maybe they were called phonograms or word families) before and, from their perspective, it didn't make much of a difference for them. They still fail all their spelling tests and have trouble reading material that is often several years below their grade level. Telling your students that the rimes are magic is a very important part of the process. If they want to know why, tell them that soon they will be able to easily recognize words because they'll be able to see the Magic Rimes inside them.

The Rime Magic sequence should be done in its entirety with any student in third grade or above (including adults) whose word-recognition grade equivalent is below 3.0. Many first- and second-grade teachers do the Magic Rimes in short lessons with their whole class. It is a fast, efficient way for first and second graders to get the critical decoding skills that they need, and it will prevent those who do not progress as easily as their peers from falling behind. It is important that each step is completed, whether the student is a first grader or a senior in high school. You will spend more time on each segment with first graders and much less time with an eighth grader in most cases. Students who are receiving special education services because of visual processing issues will need more time with Rime Magic and may need to experience the sequence even if their word-recognition grade equivalent is as high as 3.5 (see Chapter 14—Students with Learning Disabilities).

Grouping your students appropriately will enhance the success of your intervention program. I strongly suggest that you group students who score below 2.0 (word-recognition grade equivalent) separately from those who score between 2.0 and 3.0. This will allow all students to get the most benefit from the lessons. Students who score above 2.0 will dominate the chanting of the rimes and spellings and should work with others who score above 2.0. Students who score as low as .3 can be grouped with others below 2.0, and will chime in more and more as they develop skill and feel more comfortable. However, as much as possible, it is best to try to group students with others who have very similar word-recognition scores.

Preparation: You will need a stack of 35 Magic Rime Cards that have the rime printed large and in bold color so that it stands out. The Magic Rimes are two-letter, short-vowel rimes. You will find these 35 Magic Rime Cards on the DVD that is included in this book, ready for printing. Or they can be made by hand using a thick colored marker on 3 x 5 cards. It is suggested that the cards be laminated for easy manipulation. (The Magic Rime Cards can also be purchased in a laminated set from www.rimemagic.com.)

Jaime, a 37-year-old electrician who has been working with a tutor in a library for two years and making very little progress in decoding and word recognition, was tired and frustrated after hours and hours of CVC lessons. The handsome and vibrant young man was motivated to learn to read but said he could not write at all. After 20 minutes of Rime Magic, he carefully scratched out on a piece of paper, "This is fun." He smiled and asked if his tutor could do the rimes with him every day from now on. His tutor was astonished as she watched the progress he had made in 20 minutes.

The Seven Steps to Magic Rimes

Step 1 — Review Short Vowels

Step 2 — Spell One-Syllable Words With Magic Rimes

Step 3 — Add Common Inflectional Endings

Step 4 — Spell Two-Syllable Words With Magic Rimes

Step 5 — Time for Embedded Rimes

Step 6 — The Rest of the Rimes

Step 7 — The Real World of Reading and Writing

Note: *Each step in the Rime Magic sequence is demonstrated on the DVD that accompanies this book.*

Before You Begin

I have come to realize that one of the most important factors in success with struggling readers is the affective filter. Experienced teachers know that the respect we show our students is returned to us tenfold. When I begin to work with struggling readers individually or with an intervention group, the first thing I do is make direct eye contact with them and make sure that they know that I appreciate their willingness to give me a chance to help them with their reading. Older struggling readers have had many teachers who were not able to make a difference with them, many programs that did not work for them, many bad grades, many, many failures. Often, these older students have given up and are only sitting with you to get by for another day. Because reading and writing are so central to school curriculum, many of them have decided long ago that they are "stupid." They have had enough negative input to last a lifetime.

I tell my students that I know they are smart, capable students who have had some trouble learning to read, and that everyone has difficulty with something. I share with them my own problems with my sense of direction, remembering jokes or the words to songs, my difficulty throwing a ball very far. Many of the students who need reading intervention are highly skilled in other areas. After this kind of a conversation, I often see a new willingness to try and a new awareness of possibility in their eyes.

> **The Magic Rimes give struggling readers the strong foundation that they need, the foundation that has been so elusive for them in the past.**

I tell these struggling students that Magic Rimes will work, and work quickly. They will suddenly find it much easier to figure out words that have stopped them before. Because immersion rather than mastery is a goal at every step of this process, students experience no frustration as we move through the Rime Magic sequence. They receive only positive feedback, even when they make mistakes. I am confident that they will be successful, and they are. The Magic Rimes give them the strong foundation that they need, the foundation that has been so elusive for them in the past.

What You Will Need

In order to complete the Rime Magic sequence of lessons and activities with your students, you will need the following materials from the DVD:

- Short Vowel Card
- Magic Rime Cards
- Endings Card
- Embedded Rime Cards
- Master Embedded Rime Cards
- The Rest of the Rimes Cards
- Activity Sheets

- Colored pencils or colored felt-tip pens
- Pencils and paper
- Lots and lots of trade books and leveled books for guided and independent reading

Step 1: Review Short Vowels

Whether working with first graders or with middle- and high-school students, it is important to begin by making sure students know the sound of each short vowel. Older students are usually familiar with short-vowel sounds, but some struggling decoders need a quick reminder. A simple, efficient method of ensuring that students are familiar with the sounds of short vowels is described below in two parts.

> All of the cards used in the Rime Magic sequence can be found in three places:
>
> 1. Listed in the chapters of the book to be printed by hand and laminated (see above).
> 2. Printed in the enclosed DVD to be copied, cut out, and laminated.
> 3. Ordered in a complete laminated set.

Using Pictures to Reinforce Short-Vowel Sounds

Each short vowel is represented by a familiar picture. I use a picture of an apple for the short vowel sound *a*, elephant for *e*, insect for *i*, octopus for *o*, and umbrella for *u*. However, any common word that begins with one of the short vowels will work just as well. In a first-grade classroom, large pictures are displayed so that the whole class can practice briefly each morning together. For intervention groups, a card containing the pictures is kept in front of students on the reading table, so that they can refer to it as needed (see DVD).

Short Vowel Card

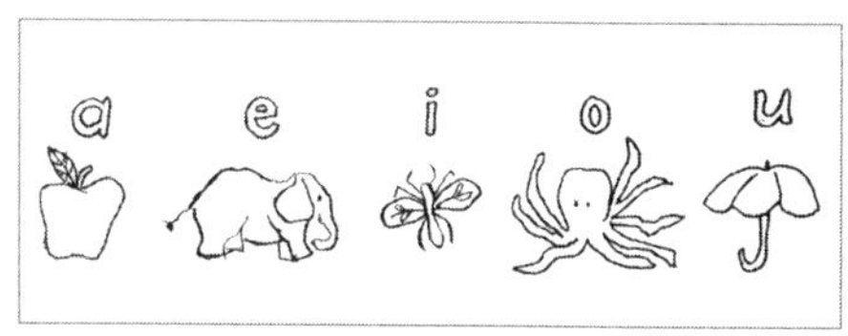

There are many ways to approach the teaching of short-vowel sounds. When I work with older students especially, I want to do this as quickly as possible, just to make sure they are familiar with the sounds. Although I often run into upper-grade students who have forgotten, they pick it up quickly when it is reintroduced. I just say, *You know that the letter* a *can say the sound of* a *like the beginning of* Amy, *and it can also say* a *like the beginning of* apple, *right?* We go through the five vowels, practicing the short-vowel sounds. While I point to each picture, we say in unison, "a, a, apple . . . e, e, elephant . . . i, i, insect . . . o, o, octopus . . . , and u, u, umbrella." Older students who are free of memory or processing issues usually need to practice the short vowels only once or twice unless they are just becoming familiar with the sounds of English as a second language. In a first-grade classroom, we leave large pictures up and practice once or twice each day for a few weeks or as long as it takes for students to feel comfortable with the short-vowel sounds. This should never take longer than a minute or two.

Using Magic Rime Cards to Reinforce Short-Vowel Sounds

After practicing briefly with the short-vowel pictures, use the Magic Rime Cards (see Table 1) to reinforce the short vowel sounds. Hold up each rime card and cover the consonant, asking students to say "a, a, apple" if the rime begins with the letter *a* as in *ap*, for example, encouraging students to refer to the short-vowel pictures if they are not sure of the short-vowel sound. Do this with a few of the rime cards so that students begin to understand (without telling them explicitly) that each rime begins with one of the short vowels.

List of Magic Rime Cards

ab	eb	ib	ob	ub
ad	ed	id	od	ud
ag	eg	ig	og	ug
am	em	im	om	um
an	en	in	on	un
ap	ep	ip	op	up
at	et	it	ot	ut

Table 1

DVD

Step 2: Spell One-Syllable Words with Magic Rimes

Recognizing Two-Letter, Short-Vowel Rimes

You will be teaching students to recognize the two-letter, short-vowel rimes in random order. These rimes form the basis of the Rime Magic strategy. It is important to introduce these particular rimes before you introduce "The Rest of the Rimes" (see Step 6). Why start with the two-letter, short-vowel rimes? Students need a chance to blend onsets and add endings to rimes when there is a consistent resulting structure to the words. The English language is often inconsistent. The support structure of keeping the rimes limited to those with two letters and short vowels will allow students to get a firm

Students need a chance to blend onsets and add endings to rimes when there is a consistent resulting structure to the words.

grip on the blending process. At the same time, they have a chance to become proficient at visualizing the onset that comes before the rime and the inflectional endings that are attached to make longer words. When the onset and the ending are visualized with the rime (in large, colored print) standing there in all its glory, students focus on the middle of the word instead of just on the beginning (or beginning and ending). They begin to realize that there is an internal structure to words that they had never noticed, and that once they see the rime separate from the rest of the letters, it is *easy to decode*. It is important that students struggling with word recognition become comfortable with focusing primarily on the Magic Rime in words that are consistent, visualizing the onset and ending in the safe environment of their small intervention group. The magic happens when this new ability transfers to real reading!

You will need a stack of 35 Magic Rime Cards, printed in bold color. They can be made using a thick colored marker on 3 x 5 cards and laminated for easy manipulation. (See Table 1 on page 20 for list of Magic Rimes.)

Or, as mentioned earlier, Magic Rime Cards can be printed from the DVD and laminated. To purchase a complete set of laminated cards, you may order the Rime Magic Card Kit at www.rimemagic.com.

The Rime Magic strategy is based on *immersion*, not mastery. If a student is just saying the rime along with you, it will become more and more familiar each time you go through the cards.

Spelling One-Syllable Words

Hold up your stack of Magic Rime Cards. Your deck of cards should always be shuffled into random order. It is important that students run into the five short-vowel sounds randomly, rather than exposing them to just short-a rimes first, for example. This will give them faster access to mastery of all of the rimes. Ask your students to say each Magic Rime with you three times in unison. You will allow at least one student in the group to begin, and then chime in with them. It is important to have them say the Magic Rime three times with you so that you can be sure that each student is saying it at least once out loud. Also, it allows the quiet, more hesitant student to have a chance to say the rime at least once. Be sure that you say the rime in unison along with your students. There is a very important reason for this: The Rime Magic strategy is based on *immersion*, not mastery. If a student is just saying the rime along with you, it will become more and more familiar each time you go through the cards. Remember, students who aren't ready to say the rimes independently are just chiming in with the rest of the group, thereby experiencing no frustration, just immersion.

TIP ~ *I usually ask my students if anyone can tell me what I mean by "in unison." We discuss keeping our voices together, softly, with no one ahead of the group.*

As you say the rime in unison with students, keep your voice just a little behind them, allowing them to recognize the rime on their own. This "wait time" is important. After at least one student starts to say the rime, go ahead and chime in, keeping your voice somewhat low. Saying each rime three times as you move through your deck of Magic Rimes, stop once in a while and ask students how to spell a one-syllable word based on the rime.

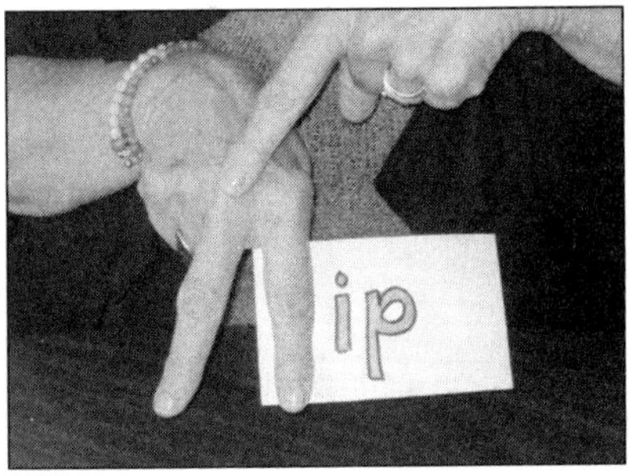

Finger placement for one-syllable word

Example: Holding up the "ip" card, say "ip ip ip" in unison with your students. Then say, *Let's spell* slip or *How do you spell* slip*?* Hold the first two fingers of your right hand pointing down in front of the rime (*ip*) to represent the onset (*s-l*) while holding the rime card with your thumb and forefinger of the same hand. For the word *strip*, hold the first two fingers before the rime (see picture). With your left hand, point to each finger representing a letter in the onset and then to each letter on the Magic Rime Card while spelling the word in unison, chiming in with your students.

Examples of One-Syllable Words with a Magic Rime

ip	slip, ship, drip, flip, trip
um	drum, strum
ot	spot
at	flat, splat
ep	step
im	swim, trim, skim
ig	twig, sprig
ad	glad
em	them, stem
op	stop, flop, shop
it	slit, split

Table 2

With beginning first graders, start with only one letter (represented by one finger) in front of the Magic Rime, spelling words such as *dip* or *rip*. But very soon, be sure to move on to two- and three-letter blends, even before you feel that most students are ready for two-

and three-letter blends. This will keep your stronger students engaged and will speed up the learning process for the rest of the class. After experiencing this immersion day after day, they will surprise you, able to spell words at a level that you might not have expected. For second graders and up, always start with two- and three-letter blends preceding the Magic Rime, unless you are working with a student with a severe language-processing deficit who needs more of a foundation. For most older students, there is no reason to start with single consonants; they will appreciate your trust in them.

TIP ~ *When spelling the word with your students, do it with a cadence, a rhythm, so that all of your voices stay together. I find that my head bounces slightly with the rhythm as we spell each letter. If you notice that your students are not keeping their voices together or are trailing off at different times, bringing your attention to the cadence will solve the problem.*

If students have any difficulty with spelling the consonant blend represented by your two or three fingers, help them hear the separate letter-sounds by stretching out the sounds of the consonants in the onset, then ask them to spell it again. This will feel easy to even the least able student, because you will be saying the letters right along with them, knowing that students, chiming in with the rest, will catch on a little more with each spelled word.

Each time you go through the Magic Rime Card deck with your students, have them spell only a few words here and there. For most rimes, just say the rime three times in unison without asking students to spell a word. Every few rimes, ask them to spell a one-syllable word using your fingers to mark the place of each letter of the onset (consonant blend). It is important that you not spell a word for each Magic Rime. If you spell a word only here and there, you will keep a pace going that generates continued enthusiasm.

What about older students?

Always have students in the upper grades spell words with two or three letters in the onset, even in your first lesson. This one-syllable word segment should take very little time (only a couple of minutes and then never again!) with older students who need Rime Magic intervention. One brief session is usually enough. It's important initially to give older struggling decoders a chance to visualize letters represented by your fingers in front of a rime. This will contribute to their ability to blend the onset with the rime as they progress through the subsequent steps of Rime Magic.

Step 3: Add Common Word Endings

s
ed
ing
er
est
y
le

When your students appear to be comfortable with the spelling of one-syllable words, visualizing the onset while seeing the rime, you are ready to introduce seven common word endings. These endings will be added to the one-syllable words that your students have become familiar with, to create two- and three-syllable words. Your older students will greatly appreciate this. It allows you to spend very little time spelling words that they associate with the primary grades. As soon as you begin spelling two-syllable words, older students realize that this technique has promise, and they perk up. You can expect to get to this point in the process within 10 minutes of the beginning of the first lesson with many of your older intervention students who do not have a serious letter confusion issue, since introducing short vowels (Step 1) and spelling one-syllable words (Step 2) often take just a few minutes. You will be amazed at how quickly your older students, who have such a hard time making their way through material far below their grade level, catch on to the blending and spelling when they spend a few minutes blending, spelling, and visualizing with a consistent rime.

You might introduce these endings by offering your students some examples and asking them to listen to the end of the word while you point to the ending. It is not important that they have mastered the sounds of these endings or even know exactly what you are talking about! This skill will deepen as you practice the spellings.

For example, you might ask:

- Do you hear the ending *er* at the end of the word *bigger*? Listen: *bigger*. Do you hear the *er*? What about *biggest*? Do you hear the *est*?
- Sometimes *y* says *ee* at the end of a word. Can you imagine the *y (pronounce ee)* at the end of *puppy*? *happy*?
- Listen to the end of the word *little*. Do you hear the *le*? What about the word *apple*?

Keep the endings where students can see them at all times. For an intervention group, you will have them in plain sight on the Endings Card on the reading table.

Step 4: Spell Two-Syllable Words With Magic Rimes

Magic Rime Card, both sides

Now you are ready to have students spell two- (and sometimes three-) syllable words using the Magic Rime Cards, your fingers representing the letters at the beginning and at the end of the word. Begin by holding up a rime card and asking students to say the Magic Rime three times in unison, as they've been doing. Then ask them to spell one of the two-syllable words printed on the back of the Magic Rime Card, letting them know ahead of time that you will be doubling the consonant in the rime.

For example, if the rime is *ad*, you could ask students to spell *ladder*.

TEACHER AND STUDENTS: (holding Magic Rime Card) "ad ad ad"

TEACHER: *Let's spell* ladder. *I climbed a ladder to reach a light-bulb. And* (pointing to the d on the Magic Rime Card) *we're going to double the consonant.*

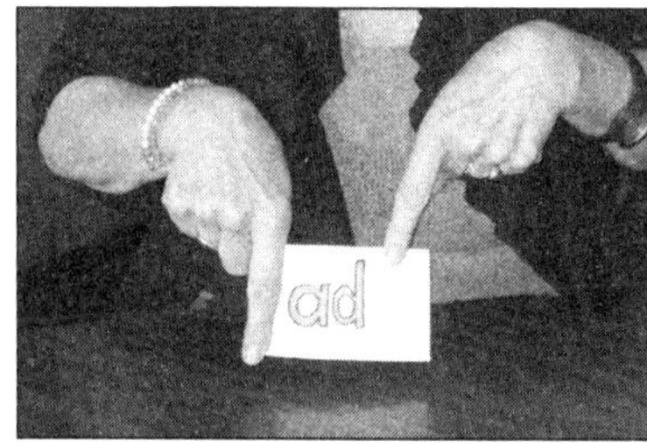

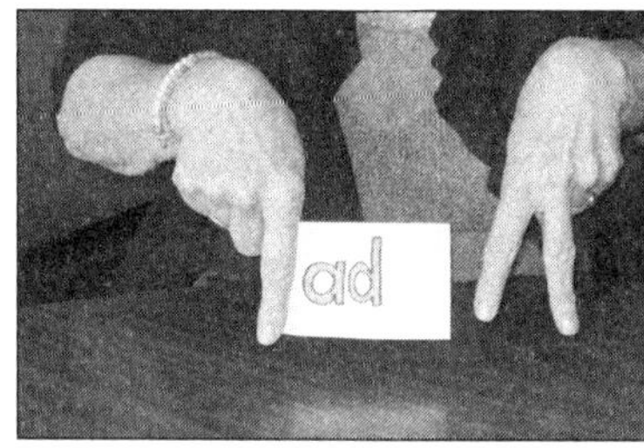

Finger placement for two-syllable word

Hold the Magic Rime Card with your right thumb and forefinger, your right forefinger representing the letter *l* and your thumb holding the card in place. As you spell the word slowly in unison with students, use your left pointing finger to identify the place where the letter l would be, right before the rime, then point to each of the two letters in the rime (*a-d*), and the place where the extra consonant (*d*) would go, finally using the fingers on your left hand to represent the letters of the ending (*e-r*). (See the DVD for a demonstration of this finger-pointing procedure.) It is important that your students visualize the letters surrounding the Magic Rime, while they see the Magic Rime standing there boldly in color.

> It is important that your students visualize the letters surrounding the Magic Rime, while they see the Magic Rime standing there boldly in color.

As you spell each word with your students, remember that you are immersing them in the correct spellings and placements of letters. It is not a test. Therefore, you will say each letter aloud with your students. If it appears that they are just following your voice and do not know how to spell the word, that's just fine. The more words you spell, the more comfortable, and then skilled, they will become. However, just as before, wait time is important. Give them a chance to try to spell the first letters of the word just a little ahead of you so that they are able to come to the spelling on their own. Just chime in with them as soon as they get started.

As you practice the rimes, saying them in unison three times each, you will ask students to spell two- and three-syllable words with you only here and there. It is best not to ask them to spell a word for every rime because you want to keep the pace brisk and the interest level high.

TIP ~ *I do not tell students a "rule" about doubling the consonant. The Rime Magic process will allow students to become aware of the need for doubling consonants and to identify when they need to be doubled. This will become clear as you move past the initial stages and into The Rest of the Rimes (see Step 6). where consonants often do not need doubling. For now, just tell students that we will double the consonant in our Magic Rime each time we add an ending. This will become automatic.*

Examples of Two- and Three-Syllable Words With a Magic Rime

ad	ladder, saddle
im	swimming, slimmer
an	planning, scanner
ug	struggle, plugged
et	better, wettest
id	griddle, skidding
up	puppy, guppy
ed	wedding, shredder
at	splatter, flattest, scattering
ip	slippery, flippers, skipping

Table 3

TIP ~ *When students have difficulty spelling an onset, just help them hear each letter as you "stretch it out" for them. Be sure to maintain a positive response. If the word is* splatter, *and the student says* s . . .l . . . , *my response is,* That's right! *Splatter begins with an s and here is the l.* Now listen, *s/p/l/ atter. Usually the student will be able to hear the missing* p *after you stretch out the onset. Remember, they are always right. Just notice where they are right, and help them with the rest! After supporting students in spelling the word, ask them to spell it again. This time they will spell it more fluently.*

When your students are comfortable spelling two-syllable words while visualizing the onset and ending, you can begin to introduce more than one ending for some of the words.

TEACHER: (holding up the Magic Rime Card *at*, saying the rime three times in unison with students) *Listen to this word:* splattering. *My baby sister was* splattering *milk all over the floor! Do you hear two endings in* splattering?

FRANK: *I hear* ing*!*

TEACHER: *Yes, I hear it too!* Splattering. *Do you hear another ending in front of* ing?

ANTONIO: er*!*

TEACHER: *Does everyone hear the* er? *Listen . . .* splatt-er-ing. *Let's spell* splattering.

STUDENTS: (with teacher chiming in, as teacher points to the three fingers representing the onset *spl*, the *a* and *t* on the Magic Rime Card, the extra *t*, the two fingers representing the ending *er* and the three fingers representing the ending *ing*): *s-p-l- a-t- t- e-r- i-n-g.*

TEACHER: *Perfect! You are so good at this! Let's spell it again!*

It is also fun to encourage students to notice when a word has two endings and the *silent e* in the first ending is dropped when the second ending is added.

TEACHER: (holding up the Magic Rime Card *ug*, saying "ug" three times in unison with students) *How would we spell* juggling? *How many endings do you hear?*

SAMMY: *Two!* le *and* ing!

TEACHER: *That's right, Sammy!* (pointing to the *le* on the endings chart) *But what happens to the* silent e *when we add the* ing?

STUDENTS: *We drop it!*

When you spell the word *juggling*, using your fingers for letter placeholders, you can make a production of dropping the *silent e* and adding the *ing*. There is much enthusiasm whenever a *silent e* is dropped.

REINFORCEMENT ACTIVITY #1

Stand-up Rimes

(recommended for Grades 1 and 2)

Purpose: This activity will reinforce students' ability to hear the rime within a two-syllable word as it is spoken aloud.

Prerequisite: Students have had practice spelling two-syllable words that contain two-letter, short-vowel Magic Rimes, using the teacher's fingers as placeholders for the one, two, or three consonants in the onset, for the extra consonant following the Magic Rime, and for the one, two, or three letters in the ending(s).

This activity can also be done with beginning first graders who have spelled one-syllable words using the Magic Rime Cards with finger placement for the onset only.

Time: 3 to 5 minutes

Materials: Magic Rime Cards

Have students sit on the rug in front of you. After practicing spelling two-syllable words using fingers as placeholders with the Magic Rime Cards, choose four students to join you in front of the class. Have each of the four students face the class, holding a Magic Rime Card chest-high so that the class can see the four Magic Rime Cards. Ask the class to pay close attention to the word that you are going to say, and to raise their hands if they know which standing student is holding the magic part of the word.

For example, you might call out the word *splatter.*

TEACHER: *My word is* splatter. *I tried not to* splatter *my paint. Raise your hand if you can tell us who is holding the magic part of* splatter (or *the Magic Rime in* splatter).

First graders playing Stand-up Rimes

A few students raise their hands.

TEACHER: *Let's see, I see five people who know . . . six, seven . . . . Okay, how about you, Kevin?*

KEVIN: (points to Julio, who is holding the Magic Rime *it) Julio!*

TEACHER: *Hmmm . . . . Let's see, Julio has the Magic Rime* it, *so the word would be* splitter. *Listen, my word is* splatter. Splatter. *Very good guess, Kevin! Who else would like to try it? Selena?*

SELENA: *I know! It's Naomi!* at!

TEACHER: (takes Naomi's card and holds it up*) Do you agree? Is* at *the Magic Rime in* splatter?

CLASS: *Yes!*

TEACHER: *Yes, that's right, Selena! Let's all spell* splatter*!* (uses fingers to represent onset and ending letters) *Selena, you can come up and take Naomi's place in front of the class. Naomi, will you hand Selena a new Magic Rime Card? Okay, here is the next word.* Biggest. *The elephant was the* biggest *animal we saw at the zoo. Who can hear the Magic Rime in* biggest? *Raise your hand and tell me who is holding the Magic Rime in the word* biggest.

Continue having students guess who is holding the Magic Rime Card and then spell each word with fingers and the Magic Rime Card. Each time a student chooses an incorrect rime, pronounce the word as it would sound with that rime. Do this with a sense of humor as if there is a joke between you, rather than treating it as an incorrect answer, and acknowledge the student for making a good guess. Most often, students will be able to do this activity fairly effortlessly after a few practice words. After each correct guess, ask the group if they agree that this is the rime. Then spell the word with finger placement as you have done before.

REINFORCEMENT ACTIVITY #2

What's My Rime?

DVD

(recommended for small-group intervention, all grades)

Purpose: This activity will reinforce students' ability to hear the rime within a two-syllable word as it is spoken aloud.

Prerequisite: Students have had practice spelling two-syllable words that contain two-letter, short-vowel Magic Rimes, using the teacher's fingers as placeholders for the letters in the onset and the ending.

Time: 3 to 5 minutes

Materials: Magic Rime Cards

If you have a small group at a reading table, distribute three Magic Rime Cards to each student, placed face-up, facing the students, for all to see. Ask your students to pay close attention to the word that you are going to say, and to tell you if they have the Magic Rime that is inside that word in front of them.

What's My Rime?

TEACHER: *If you have the Magic Rime inside the word* swimmer, *hold it up.*

Most often, students will be able to do this task fairly effortlessly. When the student holds up the card, ask the group if they agree that this is the rime. Then spell the word with finger placement as you have done before. If the student holds up the incorrect card, tell him what the word would sound like with that rime. For example, if the student holds up the Magic Rime *am* for the word *swimmer*, show them that it would say "swammer," appealing to their wonderful sense of humor. Then, repeat the question: "So . . . who has the magic part of *swimmer*?"

After taking the correct Magic Rime Card from the student and holding it up and chiming in to spell it with the group, replace the rime with another one in front of the student who produced the rime. Most often, students participating in the Rime Magic sequence become proficient at this activity after a few sessions. When the group is consistently identifying the correct rime, this activity is no longer needed.

TIP ~ *I have found that it is best to stop the game before students are ready to stop, so that they will look forward to doing it again.*

REINFORCEMENT ACTIVITY #3

DVD

Highlight the Rimes

(recommended for small-group intervention, all grades)

Purpose: Support your students' progress in visualizing the onset and the endings surrounding the Magic Rime by having students write the words, highlighting the Magic Rime. This activity will raise students' awareness of the rime within a word that has more than one syllable.

Prerequisite: Students have practiced the finger-spelling steps of the Rime Magic sequence.

Time: 5 to 7 minutes

Materials: Magic Rime Cards, lined paper, pencils, colored pencils, pens, or markers.

Give each student a sheet of paper, a colored pen or marker, and a pencil. Holding up one of the Magic Rime Cards and announcing a two-syllable word that includes that rime, ask students to write down the word using pencil for the onset, colored pen for the Magic Rime, pencil for the extra consonant, and pencil for the ending or endings. Monitor students closely to be certain that they accurately represent the Magic Rime with color and the rest of the word with pencil. Students may practice reading the words at the end of the lesson.

Example: *slippery*
sl (pencil) **ip** (colored pen) **p** (pencil) **er** (pencil) **y** (pencil)

TIP ~ *For younger students' first exposure to this activity, you might want to hold up an Embedded Rime Card so that they can see the whole word as they work. For subsequent sessions, students will write the word you say as you hold up just a Magic Rime Card.*

Students will begin to see the Magic Rime standing out in the word. I sometimes tell my older students that I want the Magic Rimes to jump out at them when they are reading. Even though this activity may seem laborious—picking up pencil, then pen, then pencil—the switching of tools makes the highlighting even more noticeable to students.

This can also be a quick independent activity after your students practice enough with you. Give each student in your group a small stack of Embedded Rime Cards to copy using pencil and colored pen. This will give you a chance to work one-on-one with a particular student in the group for a couple of minutes. Of course, the best independent activity is always reading a good book!

Student doing Highlight the Rimes

CHAPTER 5

Access to the Middle of the Word: Finishing Touches

Step 5: Time for Embedded Rimes!

DVD

When your students are consistently spelling two- or three-syllable words as you hold up Magic Rime Cards, visualizing the onset, the extra consonant, and the ending(s) supported by your finger placement, they are ready for Embedded Rimes. I tell my students, "Here comes the magic part!"

You will need a stack of 60 Embedded Rime Cards that have two-syllable words containing the Magic Rimes with one ending, and 36 Master Embedded Rime Cards with more than one ending. (See page 19 for ideas on assembling the cards.)

Hold up your shuffled stack of Embedded Rime Cards, showing the words one at a time. Tell students that you don't want them to tell you the word; instead, you want them to tell you the Magic Rime inside the word. For example, if the word is *flipper*, you want them to say "ip." Often, at first, a student will raise his hand and say "er." My response might be, as I point to the *er* in the displayed endings, *"Yes, that's a very important ending. But can you find the Magic Rime in this word?"* When a student responds correctly with "ip," I surround the *ip* with my hands so that the *ip* is all that can be seen, and join students in saying "ip ip ip." Then, without joining in with the students so that they have time to figure out the word on their own, ask them to read the word. Repeat this process with each

List of Embedded Rime Cards

ladder	scatter	little	butter	bubble
happy	letter	spinning	foggy	rubbed
paddle	peppy	winner	mommy	humming
planning	wedding	slipper	jogger	snuggle
scrabble	webbed	dripping	blogging	guppy
shatter	hemming	flipper	sloppy	puddle
splatter	settle	wiggle	stopping	struggle
strapped	petting	shimmer	hotter	muddy
apple	stepped	slimmest	spotted	funny
slammed	skidded	jiggle	juggle	running
hammer	scribble	plodding	supper	scrubbing
baggy	spitting	robbed	strumming	drummer

Table 4

Showing rime in Embedded Rime card

word. By identifying the rime ahead of time, students are surprised to find that they are able to easily blend the onset and the ending with the rime and correctly pronounce the word.

If you find that your students need a little assistance with some of the words, do not be concerned. Just assist them as needed by directing them back to the rime and allowing them to keep attempting or help them to blend it with the onset. Once they have blended the onset and rime, the ending will come easily. With just a little practice, they will become proficient at saying the rime, then the word. With many students, this ease of pronunciation will transfer automatically to their reading of connected text. For the students who need support with this transition to seeing the rimes in words as they read their books, see Step 7: The Real World of Reading and Writing (p. 39).

TIP ~ *Some students, often those who have qualified for special education services, have difficulty blending the onset with the rime, sometimes inserting a letter from the end of the word into the onset. For example, if your Embedded Rime word is* saddle, *a student might say,* "sladder," *I respond by going right back to the Magic Rime while covering up the extra* d *and the ending. When you notice that your students need assistance with any part of the word, help them by isolating and displaying just the rime, then the rime with the onset, and finally, with the ending. For more tips on assisting a student with letter confusion, see Students with Disabilities Can Learn to Decode in Chapter 14.*

When your students become more proficient at identifying the Magic Rime as you show them each Embedded Rime Card, you may begin to have them go quickly through the stack of cards, saying the Magic Rime and then the word, without bothering to say the Magic Rime three times before pronouncing the word.

Once your students feel comfortable identifying the Magic Rime in each of your Embedded Rime Cards and then saying the word, you are ready to add the Master Embedded Rime Cards to the mix. These words have more than one inflectional ending. As you hold up the cards, you can talk about and spell multiple endings. Students will notice that in words such as *snuggling* or *juggling*, the *silent e* is dropped in order to add the *ing*. Also, they might find it interesting that the silent e is often shared by two endings. Many of the younger students shout out in delight when they notice the sharing of the *e*.

TEACHER: *(holding up the Embedded Rime word* snuggled*) How many endings do you see in* snuggled*?*

TREVOR: *Two! I see* le *and* ed.

TEACHER: *And what do they have to do?*

STUDENTS: *Share the* e*!*

Teacher holds up the Embedded Rime word *juggler*.

STUDENTS: ug, ug, ug . . . juggler!

TEACHER: *And what's happening here?*

STUDENTS: le . . . er . . . *they're sharing the* e*!*

Remember, mastery along the way is not what we're after. You might be surprised how quickly students who have been stuck for years practicing CVC and CVVC words are developing proficiency with Embedded Rimes. Support your students' new success in seeing the rime within the word by having them see if they notice any of these Magic Rimes in their reading. For students who do not make this transfer right away, see Step 7 for activities that will help students see rimes in connected text.

List of Master Embedded Rime Cards

shattering	scattered	straggler	haggled
paddling	apples	splattering	splattered
letters	leggings	settled	littlest
wiggly	slippery	flippers	wiggled
jiggling	shimmering	scribbling	shimmery
robbery	sloppier	sloppiest	foggier
foggiest	buttered	snuggled	juggling
sputtering	snuggling	juggler	muddiest
muddier	bubbles	struggling	buttering

Table 5

Step 6: The Rest of the Rimes

Now that your students are able to identify the Magic Rime in a two- or three-syllable Embedded Rime word, blending all of the "chunks" together to pronounce the word, you are ready to expand the rime pool and focus on "The Rest of the Rimes." Educational researchers have created lists of rimes that are the ones most commonly found in books read by children. I derived my list (see Table 6, p. 35) from a combination of the Most Commonly Used Rimes (minus the two-letter, short-vowel rimes that are referred to in this book as Magic Rimes) that was formulated by Wylie and Durrell (1970) and the additional rimes that I have noticed over the years are helpful to students in the process of becoming proficient decoders. However, you could add to the list any rimes other than the two-letter, short-vowel rimes that are used to begin the Rime Magic sequence. Rimes with both long and short vowels are found in these lists, and they are best introduced in random order.

You will need a stack of 45 The Rest of the Rimes Cards, printed large and in bold color. They can be made using a thick colored marker on 3 x 5 cards and laminated for easy manipulation. See Table 6 (p. 35) for the complete list. Again, you can print the cards from the DVD and have them laminated or purchase the Rime Magic Card Kit at www.rimemagic.com.

The Rest of the Rimes Cards

ack	ick	ock	uck	ank	ink
unk	ame	ale	ate	ake	all
ell	ill	ight	ump	amp	ail
est	ore	ain	ice	ace	ay
oy	ine	ide	ash	ush	ish
eat	eam	ow	aw	ing	ong
oke	eet	ook	oss	ast	old
ime	ew	ipe			

Table 6

Immerse your students in The Rest of the Rimes using the same methods that were employed in introducing the two-letter, short-vowel Magic Rimes. Hold up the stack of cards, saying each rime three times with students in unison. Ask them to spell with you words that are based on some of the rimes, not all. In other words, go through the stack of cards saying each rime in unison three times, pausing to spell a word once in a while. Try to ask them to spell words that have inflectional endings as well as other suffixes, even playing with compound words, such as *nightfall*.

Here are some examples:

Using your fingers to represent the onsets and endings,

- hold up the *all* rime and ask students to spell *smaller* or *smallest*, *taller* or *tallest*, or *squalls*.
- hold up the *ight* rime and ask students to spell *brightest*, *tighter*, *nightfall*, or *lightning*.

The words you spell will often behave differently from the very consistent words based on the two-letter, short-vowel Magic Rimes. For example, when you hold up the *amp* rime, asking students to spell *trample*, they will no longer be doubling a consonant before adding the ending *le*. Because you have given your students a chance to gain mastery with two- or three-syllable words that require the doubling of a consonant, students will often automatically realize that they do not need to double a consonant in the word *trample*. Sometimes I ask students why they did not double the *p* in *trample* and they respond confidently that there are already two consonants in the word (*mp*). This is exactly the result that I want: instead of telling my students about a phonics "rule" that will most likely fly right over their heads and be immediately forgotten, I have allowed them to internalize the concept that a short vowel is usually followed by two consonants before an inflectional ending is added.

More examples:

- Holding up the *eam* rime, you might ask students to spell *streams, streamer, steaming*.
- Holding up the *ate* rime, students might at first say "at at at." My response to that is to cover the e and say, *You're right! This part says at. But when we add a silent* e, *the rime becomes* ate."

TIP ~ *Because the silent* e *does not always make the vowel long, I do not make a rule out of it. My goal is for my students to understand that vowels can be very flexible. (A group of precocious first graders once sang a song to me: "A E I O U! You just never know what they're gonna do!") I just address one rime at a time, saying, in this case, the silent* e *causes the* at *to become* ate. *Through the immersion process, students will develop a mastery of the rimes in your stack of cards.*

The importance of focusing on what they did right cannot be overemphasized. Always start with that, then add your corrective feedback in a positive way.

- After saying "ate ate ate" in unison with your students, ask them to spell *skate* and *skating*. When you spell *skating*, hold down two fingers to represent the onset *sk*, and when you add the inflectional ending *ing*, of course you will cover the silent *e* with one of your three fingers (see picture). This gives you a chance to discuss the need to drop the silent *e* in order to add *ing*.

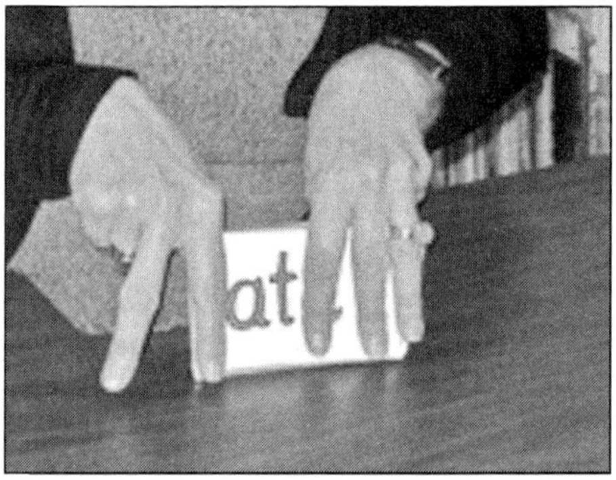

Finger placement for the word skating

REINFORCEMENT ACTIVITY #4

DVD

Rime Word Spelling

(recommended for Grade 1 and above)

Whole class (first or second grade) or small intervention group (all grades)

Purpose: This activity will reinforce students' mastery of rime placement in a multisyllabic word, enhance their ability to be aware of rime placement as they spell, and increase awareness of the separate chunks of letters inside each word.

Prerequisite: Students have completed the first five steps of the Rime Magic sequence and are able to identify the rime inside two-syllable, short-vowel words. If they have also worked with The Rest of the Rimes (Step 6), then any rime may be included in the lesson.

Time: 5 to 15 minutes

Materials: Rime Word Spelling sheet (see DVD)

Distribute a copy of the Rime Word Spelling sheet to each student. Ask students to fill in the six boxes with two-letter, short-vowel rimes. For example, you could fill the boxes with the following six Magic Rimes: *ip, at, ug, am, et,* and *ut*. If you have also spent some time on The Rest of the Rimes, you can use any rimes for this lesson. For example, you could fill the boxes with the following six rimes: *ot, art, ank, it, ight,* and *ush*. You can tell them which rimes to write in the boxes or you can ask students to choose the six rimes that everyone will use. After the six rimes are written in the boxes (all students should place the rimes in the same boxes), tell students that you will say a word and they must decide which rime is in your word. They should spell the word in the box that contains the correct rime. The first few times we do this activity, I ask students to spell one chunk at a time. For example, if the first word is *scrubbing*, I ask them to tell me what it begins with. If they respond "s," I say "s what?" I want them to tell me all of the letters in the onset (*scr*).

> **TIP** ~ *Play with the words with your students. Show them that if you choose the* up *rime for* slippery, *the word would be* sluppery. *Fun and humor work wonders with wordplay. Take some of the seriousness out of the activity and your students will look forward to the next time!*

If you choose to do this activity in a primary classroom with the whole class, you might use an overhead or digital projector. Be sure to write the words on your Rime Word Spelling sheet in front of your students, so that they will have access to immediate feedback, providing demonstration to students who need more support.

With older students, I use words with affixes as much as possible once they feel comfortable with Rime Word Spelling. For example, we might write *department* under the rime *art*. You might decide to spread this activity out over two or three sessions.

Rime Word Spelling

DVD

Spelling in the Air

(recommended for Grade 2 and above)

Whole class or small intervention group

Purpose: This activity will reinforce students' awareness and mastery of rime placement in a multisyllabic word, increase their ability to visualize letter sequence, and bring their awareness to the separate chunks of letters inside each word.

Prerequisite: Students have completed the Rime Magic sequence and are able to identify the rime inside two-syllable, short-vowel words. If they are also familiar with The Rest of the Rimes, then any rime may be included in the lesson.

Time: 5 to 7 minutes

Materials: Embedded Rime Cards

Choose a card from your pile of Embedded Rime Cards, but keep it to yourself—don't show students the word that you chose. Then ask your students to pay close attention to the word that you are going to say, and to be ready to spell out loud one of the parts of the word.

After saying the chosen word to your students, hold up one, two, or three fingers, depending on how many letters are contained in the onset of the word, while looking at one student. The targeted student will spell the onset aloud.

Next, hold up the number of fingers required to represent the rime while directing your attention toward another student. This student will spell the rime.

Then, holding up one finger to represent the extra consonant, focus your attention toward a third student, who will say the extra consonant.

Finally, as you hold up the number of fingers representing the ending, a fourth student will respond with the spelling of the ending.

Example: If the word is *splatter*:

- Focus on one student and hold up three fingers for the onset *spl*.
- Focus on a second student and hold up two fingers for the rime *at*.
- Focus on a third student and hold up one finger for the extra *t*.
- Focus on a fourth student and hold up two fingers for the inflectional ending *er*.

TIP ~ *Give students plenty of time to arrive at correct answers, or to ask a partner for help, in a way that respects and honors their participation. Each student should end his or her participation feeling smarter and more empowered than before the lesson began.*

After your students have "spelled out" the word, hold up the Embedded Rime Card so that the class or intervention group can see the correct spelling. Immediate feedback imprints the word in their memory and reinforces its structure.

More examples:

- *slippery:* *sl ip p er y*
- *flapping:* *fl ap p ing*
- *twitter:* *tw it t er*
- *gripping:* *gr ip p ing*

Once your students have become comfortable with the Embedded Rime words with two-letter, short-vowel rimes, you can work with The Rest of the Rimes. Be sure to print a word card for each word that you use so that students can see the word immediately after it is spelled.

Here are some examples:

- *splintered:* *spl int er ed*
- *trample:* *tr amp le*
- *brightest:* *br ight est*
- *stinky:* *st ink y*

The number of words you ask students to spell depends on the amount of time you want to allot for this activity. It is usually best to keep it quite short so that students do not tire of the game.

Step 7: The Real World of Reading and Writing

DVD

Magic Rime Cards may be magical, but they are not reading. As your students become proficient with the Magic Rimes, many of them will easily transfer their new ability to see rimes within words as they read independently. They will effortlessly blend the onset with the rime and see the rime pop out in front of the ending, bringing a new ease and fluency to their reading. First graders and eighth graders alike who have struggled with the daily reading curriculum and are introduced to Magic Rimes will be surprised to find themselves sailing through words that used to give them trouble.

However, there are students who do not automatically and immediately transfer these skills to connected text. They are able to easily identify the rime in a two- or three-syllable word (for example, they see the *ip* in *slippery*) but do not notice the rime in the word when they are faced with the dense body of print on the page of a book.

Here are three effective instructional strategies and one Reinforcement Activity for helping students see the rimes in connected text. Once students see you point out the rimes in these ways, they will more and more often notice this critical part of the word independently.

What Do You See?

Students who are struggling with decoding need daily practice in the act of reading. Classroom libraries should be full of high-interest, colorful, inviting books that are accessible to students.

If books are to be accessible, as many as possible should be shelved so that the entire cover can be seen and organized in such a way that students feel ownership and responsibility for enjoying and taking care of them. A fifth-grade classroom that supports struggling readers will have everything from Frog and Toad books by Arnold Lobel to *Bone* and other graphic novels.

> Students who are struggling with decoding need daily practice in the act of reading. Classroom libraries should be full of high-interest, colorful, inviting books that are accessible to students.

When I have the chance to sit down and talk about a book with a struggling decoder, I always ask him or her to read part of the book to me. This is my chance to assist the student in bringing the Magic Rimes to life within connected text, making a transition from the Embedded Rime Cards. While many students make this transition effortlessly, others need a little nudge.

When the student is reading aloud and becomes "stuck" on a word, I first of all wait to see what strategies she might employ to figure out the word. If, based on the first consonant or consonant blend, she guesses a word that makes no sense in the context of the sentence, and I see that she is continuing on despite having lost the meaning, I might stop her right there and ask if that made sense or sounded right to her. If she does try to find a word that makes sense in the sentence, I might acknowledge her for doing that and then join her in taking a closer look at the unknown word.

If the word has one of the Magic Rimes in it, this is sometimes not apparent to the student even though she is able to easily identify the Magic Rime inside any word on the Embedded Rime Cards. When the word is surrounded by lots of other words, the student's attention is spread to a much wider field. This is a good thing, as we want the largest part of attention to be focused on the meaning and story of what she is reading. However, this is also a perfect opportunity to help the reader see the rime inside the unknown word.

Let's say that the word is *wiggly*. Once we begin to look at the word, I simply say, "What do you see?" Instantly, this student will apply her newfound skills with embedded rimes and respond, "Oh, I see the *ig*! It's *wiggly*!" "Well, let's see if that makes sense in the sentence," I reply. When the student reads the sentence from the beginning, it does make sense. Very satisfying! This strategy works just as well with longer words, such as *flabbergasted*. When asked what she sees, the student will most often go right to the *ab*, figure out *flabber*, then notice the *as* or *ast* in the third syllable, and successfully pronounce the word.

Leland, a lively African-American seventh grader who began sixth grade reading at first-grade level, sat in his reading intervention classroom twitching every few seconds while engrossed in his READ 180 independent reading book. Each morning for several days his teacher had been noticing this behavior and wondered what was causing it. One morning, concerned, she sat down with him and asked, "Is everything all right? I notice you seem a little nervous. I see you jumping around in your seat while you read and I don't think you used to do that."

Leland looked up at her and said, "It's an *ip*! See?" There, on the page, was the word *flippant*. He continued, "Ms. Zinke said the Magic Rimes should jump out and slap us in the face!" This student was now reading at fifth-grade level, reading every day and at home at night, gaining confidence and a love of books. And yes . . . he did finally stop jumping!

After just a few guided opportunities to respond to the question "What do you see?" most students will begin to see the rimes on their own while reading connected text. This will be a novelty at first and then, after a while, it will become a natural part of their awareness during independent reading. First graders get the biggest kick out of this when they first discover it while reading their little predictable books during guided reading lessons and independent reading time. They squeal with delight each time they see one of the Magic Rimes jumping out at them. Reading time becomes a good kind of noisy for a while!

For some students, who need even more support at first when reading connected text, instead of asking "What do you see?" I begin with, "Look at the *ig*." That will almost always do the trick and the student will immediately pronounce *wiggly*. Before long, all I have to say is "What do you see?" And soon after, the rimes will begin to pop right out of the words.

Examples:

- **wiggly:** "Look at the *ig*."
- **cracker:** "Do you see the *ack*?"
- **nudge:** "Do you see the *ud*?" (because *udge* is the actual rime in *nudge*, you could say, "Do you see the *udge*?" but either will work just as well)

Of course, many, many words that our readers will encounter are not as regular as the ones listed above. When students are reading independently, they should not run into very many unknown words if their books have been chosen appropriately. They should be able to recognize, using grapho-phonemic, syntactic, and semantic cues, more than 95 percent of the words on the page. However, students who are reading below grade level often find themselves in an untenable situation, a sea of unknown words taunting them from the pages of a science or history textbook or a required novel in an English class. These materials are filled with words that are not the safe, warm words from the Embedded Rime Card deck. When I am reading with a student in a piece of text that is challenging, I choose one of two paths. If the text is extremely challenging, I use the TO, WITH, BY strategy (see Chapter 9, What About Fluency?). In addition, a discussion of unknown vocabulary is often required for older students, or a building of prior knowledge about the subject. If the text is only somewhat challenging, or is at the student's instructional level and he is able to identify close to 90 percent of the words, I intervene strategically as he reads aloud. Of course, I always try to encourage the student to focus on meaning first, using strategies for constructing meaning such as reading ahead of an unknown word and then getting another running start from the beginning of the sentence. But when that doesn't work, I ask the student if he can find a part of the word that is a known rime or affix, or I tell the student the pronunciation of a part of the word.

Here are some examples:

The unknown word is *endowment*. The student has already used contextual strategies and is still stuck.

TEACHER: *Do you see a prefix and a suffix?*

STUDENT: *Yes, I see the* en . . . *and* ment *at the end.*

TEACHER: *Yes, and the* o-w *in this word says* ow, *like in* cow.

STUDENT: *Oh,* en . . . dow . . . ment. Endowment*!*

TEACHER: *Excellent! Now let's read the sentence again from the beginning. Do you know what an* endowment *is? Sometimes a word is harder when you haven't heard of it before.*

The unknown word is *trouping*.

TEACHER: *The* o-u *in this word says* ou (oo).

The unknown word is *beguiling*.

TEACHER: *Do you see the* ile *hiding in there? They had to drop the* e *because of the* ing.

TIP ~ *Since the vowels in English are so flexible in the sounds that they can make, we need to teach our students to be flexible with the vowels as they read. For example, if a student looks at the word* done *and pronounces it with the* long-o *sound, finding that it does not make sense, we want him to automatically "try it another way" until it makes sense in the sentence. This is a strategy that many students discover on their own, but it needs to be taught to many struggling readers. Of course, using the example of the word* beguiling, *deciding whether to use short or long* i *will be possible only if the word* beguiling *is in the student's listening vocabulary.*

Colored Highlighter Tape

Use colored see-through tape to highlight the rime inside a few words on one or two pages of a book being read by your group of reading intervention students. Hold the book so that everyone can see the page(s) and read it together. After reading it, go back and talk about the words with the highlighted rimes.

TEACHER: *Look at the word* Madagascar. *What do you see?*

STUDENTS: *The* ad*!*

TEACHER: *Does that make it easier to read? Look at* happily. *Do you see the* ap*?*

STUDENTS: *And look at* biggest*! There's the* ig*! And the extra* g *and the* est*!*

Just a few highlighted words will make a difference with those students who have not quite begun to notice the rimes while they are reading connected text. For some of them, it is a happy discovery to realize that the Magic Rimes are not just on the cards, they exist inside every book!

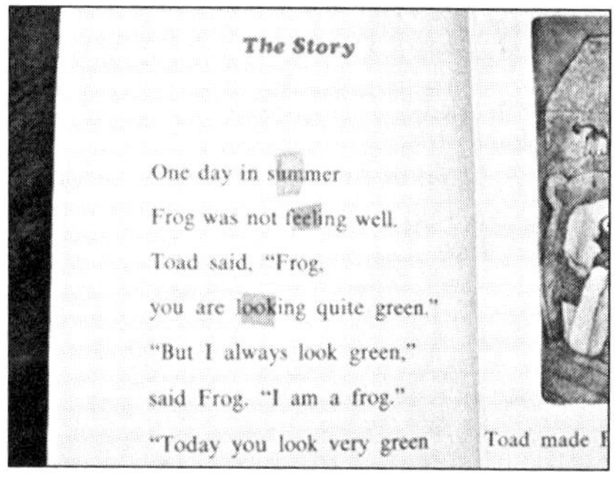

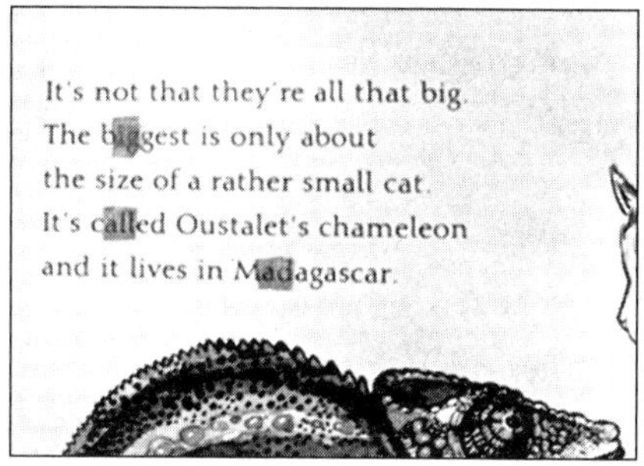

Highlight a few rimes on a page

Overhead Demonstration

All of the above strategies can be presented to the whole class using an overhead or digital projector. Recently I observed a first-grade teacher reinforcing the highlighting of rimes using her interactive whiteboard. A poem or section of a story or article can be projected and read as a class. Shared reading is always an excellent strategy to use with struggling readers in a whole-class setting. Proficient readers, along with the teacher, provide the model, and the less able readers have a much-needed chance to build word recognition and fluency in a safe environment that includes all levels of readers.

REINFORCEMENT ACTIVITY #6

Rime Hunt

(recommended for Grade 1 and above)

Whole class or small intervention group

Purpose: This activity will reinforce students' awareness of rimes within words in connected text. It is important to support students' transfer of the skills acquired during Rime Magic lessons to reading the connected text in books. Once they get some practice seeing the rimes within words in a book or poem, they will begin to automatically focus on the rime in addition to the beginning or end of an unknown word as they are reading

Prerequisite: Students have completed the Rime Magic sequence enabling them to identify the rime inside two-syllable, short-vowel words, and are familiar with The Rest of the Rimes.

Time: 5 to 10 minutes

Materials: A copy of a simple poem for each student

After enjoying a simple poem with your students and reading it together chorally, distribute a copy of the poem to each student and a copy for yourself. Ask students to focus on one word at a time, locating the rime in each word chosen by the teacher. Have students circle the rime inside the word, then write it in the right-hand margin of the page. Students can draw a box around suffixes, including inflectional endings.

Circling rimes in a Rime Hunt poem

If you choose to do this activity in a primary classroom with the whole class, use an overhead or digital projector so that everyone can see your copy of the poem. Circle and write the rimes in front of your students, so that they will have access to immediate feedback, providing demonstration for those who need more support.

I most often use simple poems, since many of the words are one or two syllables long and rimes are easy to find in them. First, of course, we enjoy the poem and have fun reading it in unison, talking about the content. Then we begin to hunt for rimes. Each student will need a copy of the poem and a pencil. Look at one word at a time with your students, searching for rimes within the word.

TEACHER: *Look at the word* Hush. *What do you see?*

STUDENTS: ush

TEACHER: *Yes, go ahead and circle* ush, *then write it on the edge of your paper. What about the word* little? *What do you see?*

STUDENTS: it

TEACHER: *Perfect! There is the* l, *the* it, *the extra* t, *and the* le! *Go ahead and circle the* it *and write it to the side.*

JEREMY: *Look at* cracker! *I see the* ack!

MARIO: *And look at* likes! *There's the* ike!

TEACHER: *Yes, and it has the ending,* s. *Just circle the* ike *and write it to the side. Then you can box the* s *because it's a suffix* (inflectional ending).

Don't worry about collecting poems that emphasize a particular rime in many of the words. It is best to hunt for whatever rimes can be found in a particular poem. Students need practice in seeing rimes in words as they appear in real literature and content area materials.

Rime Magic at-a-Glance

STEP 1: Review Short-Vowel Sounds

Keep short-vowel pictures where students can see them.

STEP 2: Spell One-Syllable Words with Magic Rimes

Practice the Magic Rimes by saying them three times each, spelling a one-syllable word only here and there, using your fingers as placeholders for the onset. Magic Rimes should be in random order.

STEP 3: Add Common inflectional Endings

Keep a list of inflectional endings where students can refer to them.

STEP 4: Spell Two-Syllable Words with Magic Rimes

Continue to practice the Magic Rimes by saying them three times each in unison with students, spelling words from the Embedded Rime list. The Embedded Rime words that you spell with students can be written on the back of the Magic Rime Cards for easy reference. Use your fingers to represent the onset in front of the Magic Rime, the extra consonant following the Magic Rime, and the ending(s). Chant the letters with a cadence to keep all voices in unison.

STEP 5: Provide Time for Embedded Rimes

Students practice identifying the Magic Rime in the Embedded Rime Cards as you hold them up. They say the rime, and then the word. After students are comfortable with the Embedded Rime Cards, add the Master Embedded Rime Cards to the mix.

- Reinforcement Activity #1: Stand-up Rimes
- Reinforcement Activity #2: What's My Rime?
- Reinforcement Activity #3: Highlight the Rimes

STEP 6: Spell Words Using the Rest of the Rimes

Spell words, mostly with more than one syllable, using The Rest of the Rimes. Reinforce the word changes that occur when endings are added. Rimes should be in random order.

- Reinforcement Activity #4: Rime Word Spelling
- Reinforcement Activity #5: Spelling in the Air

STEP 7: Explore the Real World of Reading and Writing

Help students become aware of the rimes within words as they read connected text.

- Reinforcement Activity #6: Go on a Rime Hunt

CHAPTER 6

Moving On: Multisyllabic Word Proficiency

Once your students have had enough experience with Magic Rimes along with their independent, shared, and guided reading, it's time to focus on getting proficient with multisyllabic words. Of course, one of the most effective ways to improve recognition of multisyllabic words is to become familiar with the most common prefixes and suffixes. Most reading programs found in elementary schools provide a variety of strategies for teaching affixes and morphemic elements. Many of the most common structural analysis strategies make a positive difference for students.

Here we will explore two instructional strategies that quickly and effectively provide struggling readers with a scaffolded entry into the world of multisyllabic words. The exciting news for teachers is that these strategies are easily implemented as whole-class lessons and will sufficiently reach nearly all of your struggling readers in a whole-class setting. The few students who may not need these activities as much because they are already proficient readers will enjoy them anyway and will benefit from the strong spelling reinforcement that they offer. Of course, the lessons can be reinforced with a small Tier I, II, or III intervention group for students who need more time to write the words and word parts on paper (see Chapter 12, The RTI Solution for Decoding).

When students score above 3.0 on a word recognition assessment, there is no need to do the Rime Magic lessons unless spelling is an issue. I often run through the Rime Magic sequence quickly with these students, just to make sure. With students who score above 3.0, it usually takes one or two lessons to sufficiently review Magic Rimes. The multisyllabic word strategies (Base Word Constancy and SMILES) can be done in a whole-class setting concurrently with Rime Magic lessons in grades 2–5. Students working on the Magic Rimes in intervention groups do not need to wait before participating with the whole class in multisyllabic word lessons.

DVD

Base Word Constancy

The purpose of the Base Word Constancy strategy is to help students become familiar with the morphemic structure of multisyllabic words. This strategy is done only a few times in second- through fifth-grade classrooms to introduce students to some of the most common prefixes and suffixes and the ways in which they relate to base or root words. I have found that it is much easier to focus on prefixes and suffixes when the base word remains constant and the only parts that change are the affixes. This instructional strategy is done in isolation of content area reading, unlike the SMILES strategy described in the next section. However, after the initial Base Word Constancy lessons, some teachers find it useful to refer back to this procedure when multisyllabic words appear during content area instruction.

Each student should have a Base Word Constancy sheet (see DVD). The teacher has a matching sheet that students can see on the overhead or digital projector. Begin by asking students if they know what a prefix is, leading into a discussion of affixes and base or root words. I usually talk with them about *zipping* and *unzipping* a jacket, for example, and how the prefix changes the meaning of the word. We talk about *caring*, being *careful*, or doing something *carefully*, noticing the way a suffix can change the function or parts of speech related to a base word.

TEACHER: *Today we will add some prefixes and some suffixes to the base word* port. *Please write* port *at the top of your paper where it says "Base" or "Root" . . . . Good. Now, let's look at our first word that has* port *as a base word.*

Show students the word *important.* This can be done with word cards in a small-group intervention setting or on the projector for the whole class.

TEACHER: *What is this word?*

CLASS: Important

TEACHER: *Yes, it is important that we learn to get along with each other. Do you see the prefix?*

Base Word Constancy sheet

CLASS: im!

TEACHER: *Yes,* im *is the prefix! Go ahead and write it in the first box under the prefix column on your paper. . . .* (teacher writes *im* on the projected paper to demonstrate) *Now, what is the suffix?*

CLASS: ant!

The class writes *ant* in the first box under the suffix column. Continue with each word, writing the prefixes and suffixes in the columns on each side of the Base Word Constancy sheet, and leaving the section in the middle blank.

Sample Word Lists for Base Word Constancy

form	port
information	important
formation	transportation
transforming	portable
formal	importantly
performance	export
uninformed	exporting
informal	deporting
transformation	reporter
performing	imported
transformed	transporting
informative	heliport
performer	porter

Table 7

When you come to the word *portable*, you might share with students that port sometimes means "carry" and that if you can carry something, then it is portable. My rule of thumb is that if I know the meaning of a base word or a prefix such as *ex* (out), then I share it with my students. If I don't know the meaning, I just go right on with the lesson. When the lesson is complete, I sometimes suggest to students that they might want to go online and see if they can discover the meaning of a particular prefix or root. They often rise to the challenge! The important thing is to make sure your students know that word meanings are changed by adding or subtracting morphemes (the smallest unit of meaning) and how that helps you to know what is going on when you are reading.

After all of the affixes have been written down, leaving blank spaces in the middle of the Base Word Constancy sheet, I ask the class how they think they would do on a spelling test of all of these words.

TEACHER: *Thumbs up if you think you would do great, thumbs down if you think it would be too hard, and a thumb to the side (or a side wave) if you think you might do okay and you might not.*

It is interesting how many second to fifth graders will show a lack of confidence when this question is initially asked. The fun of this lesson is to watch their confidence rise through the roof while the words are being spelled!

There are plenty of resources for structural analysis lessons. To reinforce the lessons from your basal reader teacher's manual if you are using one, lessons you have created based on your students' needs, and your Base Word Constancy lessons, you might consider using the structural analysis lessons provided in Patricia Cunningham and Dorothy Hall's *Month-by-Month Phonics for Upper Grades* (1998). The lessons based on *Nifty Thrifty Fifty* multisyllabic words are helpful in teaching students some of the more common meanings for the most-used affixes that they will run into in their reading. *What Really Matters in Vocabulary* (Cunningham, 2009), *Words Their Way* (Bear, Invernizzi, Templeton, & Johnston, 2000) and *What Really Matters in Spelling: Research-Based Strategies and Activities* (Cunningham, 2012) are also excellent resources for structural analysis strategies that will support students in reading more sophisticated text.

SMILES: Making Friends With Multisyllabic Words

Once your students are familiar with some of the most common prefixes and suffixes, they are ready for SMILES. Beginning in second grade and continuing throughout the elementary grades, I start by asking students what they think a multisyllabic word is. Often students will be able to tell you in their own way that the prefix *multi* means many and that syllabic is related to the word *syllable*, so it means words with many syllables! I tell them that sometimes these long words are the ones that are hard to figure out and are scary because they have so many letters. I let them know that SMILES will make these long words friendlier and much easier to read and spell. I ask them to smile so we can get started.

Good readers "chunk" or divide words into manageable units. In order to make long words accessible to students, we focus on separate syllables, rather than relying on the onset/rime structure of the words in the Rime Magic lessons. SMILES lessons will fit neatly into your everyday curriculum whether you are teaching math, history, science, or literature. When you encounter a multisyllabic vocabulary word in one of your content areas, set it aside for a possible SMILES lesson. This fun activity will bring students to a high level of familiarity with multisyllabic words.

The word *constitution* is an excellent example, taken from a history or political science lesson. Actually, any vocabulary word that has three or more syllables is a candidate for a SMILES lesson. You may have noticed that five of the other words in the first two sentences in this paragraph (*excellent, political, actually, vocabulary,* and *candidate*) have four syllables and would work!

The SMILES lesson is often best performed before reading literature or content-area material that includes multisyllabic words so that the focus words will be very familiar to students when they come upon them in the passage.

Each student, sitting at his or her desk, should have a blank piece of paper and a pencil. To save paper, many teachers prefer to have each student possess a small composition book where these lessons can be housed. The teacher stands in front of the room with chart paper on a chart stand, an overhead or digital projector, or interactive whiteboard.

TIP ~ *I start with one-, two-, and three-syllable words in first and second grades (see Chapter 7). After second graders have had experience with shorter words, they are ready for common four-syllable words. Third, fourth, fifth, and sixth graders, and struggling decoders in middle and high school can begin with four-syllable words.*

Let's use the word *constitution* as our first example. In my mind, I break the word into syllables that make sense to me (*con – sti – tu – tion*). The first step is to draw a box in the top two corners of my chart paper or my paper displayed digitally in front of the class, asking students to do the same. I then draw a blank for each letter of the word, one syllable at a time, saying, "*One two three SMILE, one two three SMILE, one two SMILE, one two three four SMILE.*" For each syllable, draw a "smile" under the blanks representing letters in that syllable before going on to the next syllable. Students do just as the teacher is doing. They will often repeat "*One two three SMILE,*" right after you say it, for each syllable. Your chart and their paper will look like this:

TEACHER: *My word is* constitution. (Use it in one or more sentences that are related to the use of the word in your curriculum.) *How many syllables do you think it has?* (Count the syllables by clapping each one with students.)

STUDENTS: *Four.*

TEACHER: *Yes! Keep your pencils down and let's say the word* constitution *syllable by syllable.* (Point to each syllable designated with a SMILE as you say the word *constitution* slowly, and then point and say it with students once more.)

TEACHER AND STUDENTS: (in unison) c o n - s t i - t u - t i o n

TEACHER: *Please raise your hand if you can say just the first part of the word* constitution. *I don't want you to spell it—I want you to say it.*

JEFFREY: con!

TEACHER: *Yes,* con *is the first part of the word, the prefix. I'd like everybody to write the prefix* "con" *in the three blanks over the first SMILE. When you are looking at me, then I'll know that you are finished.* (Students write.) *Let's see, who would like to spell the first part,* con, *for the class?*

JAKE: c-o-n

TEACHER: *That's right!* (write *con* on your display) *How many of you knew how to spell* con? *Great! If you need to fix any letters, go ahead and do it now. Now, who knows how to say the next part of* constitution? *Listen . . .* constitution. *Who can hear the second part?*

It is important that you say the word as you would normally, without separating the syllables, so that students are able to learn to distinguish separate syllables for themselves. Let them try to figure out the second syllable on their own, without your help.

JULIE: sti!

TEACHER: *Does everybody agree? That's right, it's* sti . . . con-sti-tu-tion. *Go ahead and try to write sti in the second SMILE. (Students write.) Who would like to spell* sti *for us? Fernando?*

FERNANDO: s-t-e

TEACHER: *Very good, Fernando. You got the* s *and the* t. (Write the *s-t* in the first two blanks in front of the class.) *Listen:* sti, sti. *Can you hear a different vowel that might go in the third blank?*

FERNANDO: i!

TEACHER: *Yes,* s-t-i *spells* sti. *Excellent! If anyone needs to change the vowel to* i, *go ahead and do it now. Now listen again to the word* constitution. *What do you hear next?*

JACOB: tu!

TEACHER: *Good. Go ahead and write "tu" in the third SMILE.* (Everybody writes.)

con sti tu tion

Distinguishing syllables is very difficult for some students who have processing difficulties associated with print. One of my favorite students is a 38-year-old adult named Clarence who was unable to hear the separate syllables at first and would not give up until he was able to do it! He was able to train his own brain to do this difficult task after much effort and determination.

Continue saying, then spelling, one syllable at a time. If a student says that *tu* should be spelled *t-o*, I say, "Yes, you are right, *to* is often spelled *t-o* when we are writing the word *to*, but is there another way we could spell *tu*?" After one of the students correctly spells *t-u*, explain to the class that in a long word, *tu* is almost always spelled *t-u*. It is important that students understand that this is a completely safe activity and that any mistake that is made is just changed right away to the correct spelling. I always tell them that mistakes are the way we learn and that's why we're here at school, to learn!

After spelling *tion* to complete the word *constitution*, it is time to highlight the affixes.

TEACHER: *Now that we have spelled* constitution, *let's box the* tion, *because it's a very common suffix* (write "tion" in the right-hand corner box at the top of the paper, asking students to do the same.) *Good. Now, what else should we box?*

SHAYLA: *The* con*! It's a prefix!* (Everyone writes "con" in the left-hand box at the top of the paper.)

Dictionaries often list two or three possible ways to divide a word into syllables together with the definition of the word. I suggest that you divide the word based on what makes the most sense to you at the moment. It is much more important that students are able to hear separate syllables one at a time than know exactly the correct division points. For example, there are several ways that you might divide the word *magnification*:

mag - ni - fi - ca - tion

mag - nif- ic - a - tion

mag - ni - fic - a - tion

Just relax and don't worry too much about where you divide the word. Your students need to start seeing these multisyllabic words in bite-sized pieces!

At this point, there is a decision to be made. You can decide to:

- go on to another word, taking it through the same steps,
- move on with your content-area or reading lesson, or
- continue with the lesson, asking students to spell derivations from the same root or base word (see below).

Some multisyllabic words lend themselves well to playing with derivations. Let's say that you have just completed the SMILES lesson above with the word *conversation*. You and your class have identified and spelled each separate syllable and boxed the prefix *con* and the suffix *tion* at the top of the page. Now it's time to spell other words derived from the base word *verse*.

TEACHER: *Please draw a line below the word* conversation *on your paper. Try to spell* converse. *If I was having a* conversation *with Jeremy, that means I had decided to* converse *with him. Spell* converse *on the line without breaking it into syllables*. (Students write "converse" on the line as best they can.)

con ver sa tion

____

TEACHER: *Who would like to spell* converse *for us?*

SHELLEY: c-o-n-v-e-r-s

TEACHER: *Excellent, Shelley, you got all of the letters except one. What letter do you think might go at the end?*

SHELLEY: *The silent* e!

TEACHER: *Yes! Everyone go ahead and add the silent* e *if you don't have it. Now, draw another line on your paper and try to write "conversing." Jeremy and I were having a conversation so we were* conversing. *Go ahead and write "conversing."* (Students write the word *conversing* on the second line.)

con ver sa tion

converse

conversing

TEACHER: *Who would like to try to spell* conversing *for the class?*

MARISSA: c-o-n-v-e-r-s-i-n-g

TEACHER: *What happened to the silent* e*?*

CLASS: *We dropped it when we added the* ing*!*

ANTOINE: *Teacher, what about my shoes?* Converse*!*

TEACHER: *Yes, Antoine! There's another meaning for this word. Good thinking. Can anyone use* converse *or* conversing *in your own sentence?*

Most teachers in upper elementary who have woven SMILES into their curriculum have found that they can only do short lessons weekly, choosing from several options. One day you might do a few multisyllabic content-area words with SMILES, and on another day only one word with a derivational study. If you have extra time, you might do one or two or three words followed by Word Juggling (see Chapter 7, Reinforcement Activity #7). In this activity, as further reinforcement of the syntactic use of one of your word derivations, you might play with one of your multisyllabic words in flexible sentences. Students can work with a partner to come up with five sentences using *conversing* or *constitution*, placing the word in five different positions. Older students find this activity challenging and fun. Start with five-word sentences and slowly (every few weeks) increase the number of words. Your students will greatly increase their proficiency and fluidity around word usage and sentence construction, while reinforcing their spelling of multisyllabic words.

Example: Use the word *conversing* in three different positions in sentences with 16 words.

Position 1: Conversing with my girlfriend on the phone is what I like to do in the evenings.

Position 2: After conversing with my mother, I decided to bake extra brownies for the party tomorrow night.

Position 5: I was hoping that conversing with my advisor would help me to pass my math class.

SMILES using math vocabulary

When you begin to include these activities in your language arts curriculum consistently, you will find that your students will increase their proficiency with multisyllabic words, whether they are reading or spelling them. When they are reading and come across a word that might have thrown them in the past, they might take a closer look at it, noticing the "little puppies" (syllables) rather than being afraid of the entire multisyllabic word—what Alfred Tatum likes to call the "big dog" (Tatum, 2005). And when they are writing, they will be more inclined to use multisyllabic words, listening to one "puppy" after another and writing them down. Your struggling readers will develop confidence that they didn't know they had. And that, of course, leads to fast success.

One day while I was demonstrating Base Word Constancy and SMILES lessons in a second-grade classroom in San Lorenzo, California, a little girl with a splash of tiny braids aiming in every direction had a hard time sitting down to focus on the lesson for the first minute or two. She had just tipped a chair over as I walked into the room and appeared to be looking for ways to entertain herself during this new teacher's lesson. But a couple of minutes into the listing of prefixes and suffixes, she was hooked, staying with me until the end of a 45-minute period. This was much longer than I would normally have second graders stay in their seats focusing on long words, but I had seven teachers in the back of the room observing the lesson, and this was our only chance to complete the demonstration.

When the lesson was over and the children began filing out to recess, the little girl looked up at me and declared, "This was fun! Funner than recess! I can spell those words!" As her girlfriends escorted her out the door, she repeated over and over, "This was even funner than recess!"

CHAPTER 7

Spelling in a Nutshell

Spelling is an issue for many of us, especially those of us learning to spell in English! Because the words we use in English are derived from so many languages and the spellings are often inconsistent, many of our students struggle to spell correctly in their writing. Of course, those of us who were blessed with a strong visual memory related to the printed word become better and better spellers, rather effortlessly, as we read more and more books and magazines and articles filled with print. However, many of our students, enjoying other strengths, do not have a strong visual memory and find the inconsistencies of English spelling akin to a minefield of potential misspellings waiting to happen!

Getting Started

After years of working with students who find spelling a challenge, I have found that it is best to first give students a strong foundation in the regular spellings of short-vowel words. Remember McCracken Spelling (McCracken, 1996)? That's an excellent way to start in first grade, scaffolding the spellings by asking students to draw lines for letters and then fill them in with letters that they hear when a word is pronounced.

TEACHER: *Draw three blanks on your paper (or whiteboard). My word is* hat. *In the blanks, write the letters you hear.*

Some first graders might only hear the *h* and are acknowledged when they write "h" in the first blank space. Some might hear the *h* and the *t* and write them in the first and third

Student doing McCracken spelling

blank spaces. And others might hear all three letters and fill in all of the blanks. As this process is repeated, more and more students will be able to hear all of the sounds. Because this is highly participatory and hands-on, young spellers make fast progress. You can move on to four- and five-letter one-syllable words.

As you begin to introduce the Magic Rimes in first or second grade, it becomes more and more important to refer to a rime as a rime and to stop treating each letter separately. Students need to see the onset and the rime as clusters or "chunks" of letters. You might have your students draw five blanks and then try to write the word *stamp*. When you ask students to spell the word right after they write it, giving them immediate feedback, ask them what the word "starts with." Your students will begin to understand that you are looking for the entire onset (*st*) at once, so the responding student, rather than saying "s," would say "st." It is important that they see the word as consisting of separate chunks rather than a string of separate letters.

TEACHER: *Draw four blanks on your paper.* (Students write _ _ _ _ .)

TEACHER: *My word is* flat. *What does* flat *start with?*

CAMILLE: fl

TEACHER: *Yes,* flat *begins with* fl! *And what rime do you hear in* flat?

CLASS: at!

TEACHER: *Yes,* at *is the rime! Please underline the* fl *and circle the rime* (at).

This strategy of filling in the blanks for one-syllable words, marking the onset and rime as separate chunks, coupled with the sequence of Rime Magic lessons (see Chapters 4 and 5), will provide a strong foundation for spelling one-, two-, and three-syllable short-vowel words. This critical foundation for spelling can be built upon by the Reinforcement Activities in Chapters 4 and 5 that require students to spell words in highly scaffolded, teacher-led activities.

DVD

Long Vowel Spelling: The End of Long-Vowel Confusion

The short vowels, of course, are the easy part when it comes to spelling. English short vowels are completely consistent (if you stick to one part of the country). It's the long vowels that cause all of the spelling problems. But take heart—there is a solution! I call it Long Vowel Spelling. After working extensively with students who have qualified for special education services, and many who haven't, students who find spelling to be especially challenging, I have come to the conclusion that English spelling begins to make sense when we can see the whole picture. Some basal reader programs begin to show students that long vowels can have different spellings, but I believe we need to go further and give our students the entire context for the varied spellings of our English long vowels, allowing them a full perspective. Although literacy researcher Theodore Clymer (1963) made it clear to us that most English spelling rules are rife with exceptions, it is also true that many consistencies can be found when we look at all of the spellings of a particular long vowel on a single page.

Long Vowel Spelling can begin in the second half of first grade and continue through the elementary grades. If all of the primary grade teachers in a particular school do Long Vowel Spelling on a regular basis, maybe once every week or two, for example, the need for this instruction will diminish for students in the upper elementary grades. If it has not been done in the primary grades consistently and there is much long-vowel spelling confusion in upper-grade classrooms, Long Vowel Spelling will make a striking difference in Grades 4 through 6.

Begin by passing out a Long Vowel Spelling sheet (see DVD) to each student or by having upper-elementary students draw the lines for nine boxes on a blank sheet of paper or a page in a composition book. You will use the same Long Vowel Spelling page with your overhead, digital projector, or interactive whiteboard, or, if you are more like me, you might choose to use a chart stand and to draw the lines each time you do the lesson. Each time you do this activity, you (or your students) will choose one of the five long vowels. I usually like to start with the long-vowel sound *a*, and we write the letter at the top of our papers. Next, I tell students that we will be spelling words that have the sound that long *a* makes.

TEACHER: *I would like everyone to think of a word that has the sound of* long a *in it, like the sound you hear in* play *or* today. *Not short* a *like you hear in* apple. *Just* long a, *where the* a *says its own name.*

Students begin to raise their hands to share a word with the class.

MOLLY: rain!

TEACHER: *Thank you, Molly! I'm going to write* rain *in the first box on my paper.* (Teacher and students write the word *rain.*) *What part of the word* rain *says "a"?*

Several students call out "*ai!*"

TEACHER: *That's right! So we will write* "a-i" *above the word* rain. *Who's got another* a *word?*

JAMES: today!

TEACHER: *Yes, James, and where should we put it? Is it an* "a-i" *word?*

STUDENTS: *No! A new box!*

TEACHER: *Yes!* (Writes *today* in the second box on the page.) *What part of* today *says "a"?*

STUDENTS: *a-y!*

TEACHER: *Good!* (Everyone writes "ay" above the word *today*.) *Who has another long* a *word?*

TREVOR: Alligator!

TEACHER: *You're right, Trevor,* alligator *has the sound of* a *in it. Where should we put it?*

TREVOR: *It has two* a*'s in it! But the first one says* a *(short* a*)!*

TEACHER: *Exactly! The second* a *in alligator says* a, *long* a. *Where do you think it goes?*

ANTOINE: *Lonely* a!

CLASS: *Yes, lonely* a!

TEACHER: *Yes, we need a box for* a *all by itself! Lonely* a!

TEACHER: *How about you, Dustin?*

DUSTIN: *snake!*

TEACHER: *Yes, now where should we write* snake*?*

STUDENTS: *New box!*

TEACHER: *And which part of* snake *says* a*?*

MARIA: a *with a silent* e!

TEACHER: *Yes, we'll write a_e above* snake.

HECTOR: *How about* train*?*

TEACHER: *Where shall we put it?*

CLASS: *With* rain!

Students will enjoy providing long-*a* words and filling in their boxes along with the teacher as long as the pacing stays brisk. Continue filling in words and identifying which part of the word says "a," writing that part at the top of the category box. It is very important to keep up the pace in this activity. Do not give in to the temptation to take advantage of every teachable moment. Just keep going. This, too, is an immersion activity; mastery is not important at this stage. As your students get familiar with the activity, they will become better and better at thinking of words and will more and more easily know where to place them. At first, many of them will just copy you and each other until they become more confident. Mastery comes easily, with practice.

Long Vowel Spelling

Each day that you decide to do this spelling activity, choose a different long vowel, starting over each time. I have found that it does not work to add on to these long-vowel pages. Adding on becomes a very different activity. Students find it much more interesting to begin all over again for each lesson. You will not necessarily put words into all nine category boxes each time. Sometimes you will write words in just four or five boxes and other times you might need to make room for eleven or twelve boxes! (Think about the word *beret*, a French word that says "long *a*.") Just do a different vowel each time and your students will feel more and more comfortable and confident with each lesson. Some teachers like to keep the charts up in the room as a spelling reference but take one down when it's time to do that particular vowel again.

TIP ~ *I include the sound of* ew *in* few *and the* eau *in* beautiful *in the Long-*u *chart along with the* oo *in* boot *and the* ue *in* blue. *When we do the Long-*u *chart, we group the* ew *sound in* few *and* grew *together in the same box, for the sake of simplicity.*

At first, some students see the many spellings of one vowel sound as somewhat daunting. One of my very studious seventh-grade boys, who had language processing issues as well as the challenge of learning English as a second language, slammed his hand down on the table after we finished our first Long-*a* chart.

"Ms. Zinke!" he shouted. "No wonder I can't spell!"

However, once we had completed all five of the long vowels two or three times over the next few weeks, all of my students began to see patterns and to become familiar with the spellings of many of the words. It appears that having students generate the words themselves gives them ownership of the interesting patterns of English orthography. Although we had not yet attempted a formal study of the transference of spelling to their writing, I began to notice a marked change in spelling accuracy in their first drafts. Seeing the whole picture appears to help us make sense of the intricacies of English spelling!

REINFORCEMENT ACTIVITY #7

Word Juggling

DVD

(recommended for Grade 1 and above)

Whole class or small intervention group
(This activity is adapted from an excellent strategy created by Leif Fearn and Nancy Farnan, introduced in their book *Interactions: Teaching Writing and the Language Arts*, to reinforce spelling words.)

Purpose: This activity will allow students to become more flexible in their use of words in structuring sentences when they engage in their daily writing. In addition, it is a fun and challenging way to practice targeted spelling words.

Prerequisite: None

Time: 10 to 20 minutes

Materials: Paper and pencils

Choose a word that is relevant in some way to the experiences of your students or the content in your classroom. If it's raining, you might choose *rain*. If you are studying dinosaurs, you might choose *dinosaur* or *stegosaurus* or *fossil*.

If you begin this activity in first grade, begin with a very common word, such as *rain* or *pencil* or *book* or *shoes*. On a windy day, ask your first graders to orally give you a sentence that has the word *wind* in it, and the sentence can have only four words. Not three, not five, just four. Be sure to let students know that they can add endings to the word. I usually write wind and windy on the chart to show all of the possibilities. *(If you use the word* rain, *print the words with their inflectional endings:* rains, rained, *and* raining *where your students can see them.)*

JOSEPH: I like the wind.

TEACHER: *Yes, Joseph, that's a sentence.* (write the sentence in front of the class.) *Now,* (say the sentence pointing to each of your four fingers) *who can tell me which position* wind *is in—first, second, third, or fourth?*

LYDIA: *It's in fourth position!*

TEACHER: *Yes, so I'm going to circle* wind *and write a number 4 over it.*

4
I like the (wind.)

FRANCO: *I've got one!* I don't like the wind.

TEACHER: *That's a very good sentence, Franco. But let's count the words:* . . . I . . . don't . . . like . . . the . . . wind. *How many is that?*

CLASS: *Five!*

TEACHER: *How can we make Franco's sentence have only four words in it?*

SAMMY: I don't like wind*!*

TEACHER: *Yes, that will work! I'll circle* wind *and put a 4 over it. Now, can anyone think of a sentence where* wind *is in a different position, not fourth?*

CELIA: The wind is cold.

TEACHER: *Yes, Celia.* (writes Celia's sentence on the chart). *Which position is* wind *in?*

CELIA: *Second!*

TEACHER: *Perfect! I'll circle* wind *and put a 2 over it.*

4
I like the (wind.)

4
I don't like (wind.)

2
The (wind) is cold.

Students throughout the classroom are busily counting words on their fingers, trying to come up with *wind* in a different position.

TEACHER: *How about first position or third position?* (hands go up)

Before long, without too much coaching, we have wind in all four positions.

3
It is windy today.

1
Wind is blowing leaves.

Another way to approach Word Juggling is to provide students with a sheet of paper that provides a blank space for each word in the sentence. Students work with a partner to fill in the sentences (see Word Juggling sheet on DVD).

When I use Word Juggling with students above first-grade level, I do not begin orally, writing their sentences on a chart as I do in first grade. I ask students to write the sentences from the very first lesson beginning with five-word sentences and moving to higher numbers throughout the school year. They do the best they can, and I see improvement each time we juggle words. During the first few lessons, whether I have second or seventh graders, I draw attention to capitalization and punctuation right away.

TEACHER: *Write a sentence that has six words in it, using the word* dinosaur *or* dinosaurs.

JAKE: Dinosaurs loved to eat smaller animals.

TEACHER: *Thank you, Jake. What position is* dinosaur *in?*

JAKE: *First position.*

TEACHER: *Yes, go ahead and circle it and put a* 1 *over it. Did you start with a . . .*

JAKE: *Capital? Yes! And I ended with a period!*

TEACHER: *Fabulous! Who has* dinosaur *in a different position?*

When I was working daily with fourth and fifth graders who were in my Resource Specialist Program in Hayward, California, we began with five-word sentences, and when my students were ready, moved on to six-, seven-, eight-, and nine-word sentences. Their writing improved dramatically with their competence at moving words around within sentences and experimenting with sentence structure. Sometimes they had to add adjectives and prepositional phrases in order to make the words fit, and they began to discover that they could write with much more sophisticated language structure. When I moved on to middle school in Berkeley, my seventh-grade RSP students began with five-word sentences and moved all the way to sentences with fourteen words. In order to do this, they had to become proficient at bringing in dependent clauses. Journal and essay writing became much more interesting!

> **TIP ~** *Work with students to set up a little graveyard for words that make sentences less interesting, such as* very very, really, *or ending sentences with* too *just to get an extra word in. Use words that are relevant to your curriculum and encourage students to use interesting vocabulary along with the target word.*

LISA:	My (pencil) [2] splintered when I pressed too hard.
TEACHER:	*Lisa, what interests me about your sentence is the vocabulary words you added to make it more exciting. Can anyone tell me what interesting vocabulary Lisa used in her sentence?*
JESSE:	splintered *and* pressed*!*

See DVD for a sample Word Juggling sheet that can be used as fun family spelling homework or in class partner work.

Independent Reading: The Key to Spelling Improvement

We only need to look at the research gathered by Steven Krashen (2004) to see that the key to spelling improvement is lots of time spent reading self-selected material at one's independent reading level. When I observe student progress in schools that honor independent reading time and provide classroom libraries with a range of interest and readability in each and every classroom, I see children losing themselves in the world of stories and exciting content. At the same time, their spelling and vocabulary knowledge are improved daily as they see words appear over and over in different contexts, making a significant impact on both reading and writing proficiency.

CHAPTER 8

Decoding Happens in Meaningful Context!

We cannot overemphasize the importance of developing proficiency in the use of context to help with decoding while engaged in reading. Although it is true that many students who struggle with decoding have strong comprehension and do a great job of using the context to help them compensate for their lack of skill in recognizing or decoding words, there are many others who do not automatically use context as they try to figure out words as they read. Many times, decoders will struggle valiantly with the letters of a word, having no idea what else to do. It is imperative that we work with these students to give them a tool kit of strategies to use as they read, especially if letter sequence gives them trouble. I will share three of the strategies that I have found most helpful for teaching students to use context and their own prior knowledge about what they are reading to help them make sense of print, rather than simply over-relying on grapho-phonemic cues.

The Cloze Technique

For decades reading teachers have been using the cloze technique to help their students to rely more on context clues. I usually begin by taking a few words out of a familiar passage or poem and asking my students to try to figure out what words might work in the blank spaces. Because I believe it is critical that struggling readers not struggle during their intervention time, we do the cloze exercise together as a group until students feel comfortable enough to try it with a partner. I do not ask them to do it alone until they request it after plenty of guided practice. Our conversations about words that might work both syntactically and semantically in the blanks are rich and powerful for the students. They discover that only certain kinds of words will work in a particular context, and when they read, they begin to share with each other how they have used a combination of decoding and contextual clues to figure out an unknown word.

Strategy Logs

Using Strategy Logs with my intervention groups has proven to be a powerful way to encourage flexible thinking and problem solving while reading connected text. I usually begin with everyone reading a copy of the same book that is somewhat above his or her independent reading level. I want the book to have one or two words on each page that stump my students so that they have to do some problem solving. Each student has a Strategy Log (a small booklet with blank pages in it) and small pieces of see-through colored highlighter tape. Everyone reads independently, and each time they have to stop and figure out a difficult word, they cover the word with colored tape, noticing how they figured it out or how they tried to figure it out. They keep reading until it is their turn to sit at the head of the table with me, bringing their book and Strategy Log along.

A group of sixth graders reading far below grade level who were in my Resource Specialist Program in an elementary school in Hayward, California, chose a beautifully illustrated copy of *Peter Rabbit* by Beatrix Potter. When Antoine came to sit next to me, I asked him which part of the book he would like to read to me. As he read, he talked with me about how he figured out the words that were highlighted by the colored tape. This was my chance to share the language of strategic readers with him just at the points where he needed it.

ANTOINE: *I was stuck on the word* fluttered *and I saw* bird *so I went back and looked at the* ut *and I got it.*

TEACHER: *So, when you were stuck on* fluttered, *you read ahead until you saw the word* bird *and you realized that the word probably had something to do with the bird! And I love the way you went back and looked at the Magic Rime in the word. Go ahead and write in your Strategy Log about the strategies you used to figure out the word* fluttered. *Great job!*

As Antoine began writing a sentence or two about the strategies he used, I asked another student to read with me. Before Antoine returned to his regular seat at the table, he read his Strategy Log description to me. I have discovered that asking students to write down the strategies they use—after discussing the strategies with their teacher—helps students begin to use these strategies more automatically in their independent reading—something we definitely want to see. One day, after Antoine had filled three-quarters of his Strategy Log with short write-ups, he rushed out of his regular sixth-grade classroom during silent reading without bothering to ask permission from his teacher. He then slammed into the resource room with his book while I was working with a group of fourth graders.

ANTOINE: *Ms Zinke! I'm doing it! I'm figuring out the words! It's easy!*

Then he ran back to class, arriving just as his teacher was calling the office to check on him.

Strategy Conversations

The best strategy of all, of course, is the simplest! When I sit with one of my students, listening to him read, I have the perfect opportunity to intervene when it is appropriate, in such a way that he can see beyond the strategies that he normally uses. When a student is reading and substituting words that retain the meaning of the passage, I do not intervene. But when he substitutes a word that doesn't work in the sentence, and if he keeps reading without ever going back to self-correct or to attempt to figure out why it didn't make sense, I will interrupt him to ask, "Did that sound right to you?" or "Does that make sense?" Sometimes struggling readers have been in classrooms where there is so much emphasis on phonics instruction that meaning-based strategies are not sufficiently brought to students' attention. Conversations about the importance of text making sense should begin in kindergarten. We must never forget that reading is constructing meaning. *Reading IS comprehension.*

CHAPTER 9

What About Fluency?

Two Misconceptions

Fluency has been a hot topic in reading education recently and has generated much controversy. Is it important to help our students develop fluency in their reading? Of course! I have always considered fluency an important part of reading instruction for both proficient readers and for students who struggle with reading. However, there are two misunderstandings that are affecting the language arts curriculum and assessment that are mandated in many of our schools, especially in the urban school districts.

First, some policy makers appear to believe that fluency has more to do with comprehension than it actually does. They believe that proficient reading is the ability to read words rapidly and accurately, resulting in comprehension. My experience, after more than 40 years of working with and observing children learning to read, tells me that reading is about constructing meaning, making sense of text. The problem solving involved in my own reading slows me down at times. Young children, new to the reading process, have even more problems to solve as they make their way through text. I expect that they would slow down as they try to make sense of what they are reading. The timed oral "fluency" tests that are ubiquitous in our schools these days are penalizing students for their attempts to comprehend what they are reading. *These tests are often given without any discussion of the text, and students are encouraged to read as fast as they can to get a higher score.* Comprehension is not a result of fast, accurate reading; rather, it is more likely the other way around. Fluency (appropriate flow) is enhanced when students read lots of books and other reading materials at their independent reading level after becoming proficient at making sense of text at that level.

A second and related misconception about fluency in reading: timed readings are the best way to measure a student's reading fluency, or even reading proficiency. Teachers in elementary schools all over the country are being required to encourage their students to speed through pages of text on a regular basis. Stopwatch in hand, three or more times each year, teachers are asking students to "read" a passage as fast as they can without self-correcting or talking about what they read afterward. Often the students are informed of their scores and the object of this "reading" test is to get a higher number of words read correctly in a minute. When I ask teachers why they don't ask students to do a retelling afterward, they tell me that the comprehension part of the test is optional and that they don't have time to include a retelling for each student. Reading in these schools has become about speed and accuracy, with comprehension a casualty. Even more worrisome, some urban school districts are requiring teachers to give timed fluency tests every two weeks to all students who receive intervention in each school's Learning Center. Teachers are frustrated when they have little time to provide instruction for the students who need it most.

When I go into a school and administer an Informal Reading Inventory, including a word-recognition test, a miscue analysis, with a retelling and/or comprehension questions, I find that many of the students have good word-recognition scores but are unable to comprehend at grade level. In one particular inner-city school, more than one-fourth of the fifth graders were reading at first- and second-grade levels based on an evaluation of their comprehension. They were flying through the passage at lightning speed and had very little idea of what they had just read. They had been trained to go as fast as possible and not worry about what they were reading. Students at many schools are now being rewarded for speed and accuracy, sacrificing comprehension and the love of reading. Given that there is no reading without comprehension, and given that the teachers and administrators in these schools want to do well by their students, there might be a big payoff in giving these assessment practices further thought.

What Is Good Fluency Instruction for Struggling Readers?

The first thing that I tell my students about reading fluency is that it is not about speed, but rather about appropriate rate. I particularly like the way Alan Flurkey talks about fluency in *The Truth About DIBELS* (Goodman, 2006). He prefers to call it *reading flow*, with reading speeding up and slowing down as readers construct meaning and make sense of text. The definition of fluency that most matches my experience with developing readers is the following: Reading accurately with expression, appropriate speed, and full comprehension (Allington, 2009b).

What is the best fluency instruction for students who are reading word by word or without a comfortable flow? It is my belief that struggling readers benefit most from demonstrations of fluent reading and from the gift of plenty of time and interesting books for guided and independent reading. Good fluency instruction can be accomplished in many exciting ways in the classroom and in small reading-intervention groups.

Shared Reading

When struggling readers are surrounded by the voices of more-proficient readers, the stress is gone and they can just chime in with the rest. The last thing we want to do with our struggling readers is raise their stress levels by putting them on the spot and asking them to read material aloud that is not within their independent reading level. Shared reading is an effective way of giving less proficient readers a chance to practice in a safe environment. This can be done with Big Books or by putting poems or segments of print on a digital projector for all to see, everyone reading together in unison. In a small reading-intervention group, shared reading works the same way. Everyone can see the print, and the story, poem, or content area material is read chorally, the teacher's voice demonstrating good pacing and intonation.

Repeated Reading

Some struggling decoders are just very slow in processing text. Some of the students that I have tutored have benefited from the repeated reading of the same interesting passage several times. In this way, confidence is built as the student sees improvement each time the selection is read. However, I join Dr. Richard Allington (2009b) in cautioning against the long-term use of repeated reading for students in intervention groups. There is a time and a place for repeated reading when a student needs a jumpstart at a particular level, but it is a much more powerful solution to support struggling readers in reading independently every day in "just right" text for extended periods of time.

Is there a place for timed readings? When teachers regularly time students' reading, comprehension is often compromised. However, I have seen improvement in the fluency of struggling readers when they use stopwatches themselves to measure speed. This can be a useful gimmick to get them to practice a short selection over and over to increase fluency. When I find myself in a room with students who are timing themselves, I talk to them about what fluent reading sounds like. I demonstrate the varied pacing that I use as I read different kinds of material or as I slow down to make sense of something I didn't understand. I show them what good expression and intonation sound like and of course, we discuss the importance of being able to talk about what they have just read. We need to be sure students understand that fluency is not synonymous with speed!

Most important, repeated reading with or without a timer should be limited to the time it takes to solve a particular student's fluency issue. It is a grave mistake to apply the same repeated reading regimen indiscriminately to all struggling readers (Allington, 2009b).

TO/WITH/BY

TO/WITH/BY is my favorite way to support struggling readers in gaining fluency and building decoding skill in the process. This strategy can be used with the whole class, in a small group, or with an individual student. It is important to use material that is highly interesting to the student. When I tutor a student who is reading far below grade level, I always ask her what she would like to be able to read. One third-grade girl who was struggling with decoding at a first-grade level told me she wanted to be able to read the original Nancy Drew books that her father read to her at night. We read one paragraph at a time in the following way: First, I read it TO her, then asked her if she wanted me to read it to her again. When she indicated that she was ready, I read the same paragraph WITH her in unison, as many times as she wanted. Finally, when she was ready, she read the paragraph to me (it was read BY her). By this time, she had memorized parts of it and she knew quite a bit about what was coming. In other words, the paragraph had become very predictable. Of course, when she was able to make her way through the paragraph without my assistance, her confidence soared.

Years ago, when I was the resource specialist at an elementary school in Hayward, California, two fifth-grade students entered our school late in the year. One boy was a member of a royal family from an island in the South Seas, the other recently from the Philippines. Both boys were learning English as a second language and had qualified that year at their previous schools for special education services due to language-processing issues. Although they were placed in fifth-grade classrooms, they were both reading at first-grade level.

One of the first things I did after assessing them was ask them what they would like to be able to read. They were both wild to be able to read Harry Potter and both had seen the first movie. I worked with the school's reading specialist, Jennifer Jones-Martinez, to set up a few minutes a day for TO/WITH/BY, beginning with the first chapter of *Harry Potter and the Sorcerer's Stone,* by J. K. Rowling. Jennifer read one paragraph at a time to them, they read it with her in unison, and then practiced reading it as partners and finally by themselves. We supported the effort in the Resource Room. Within a couple of weeks, both boys were able to read the first chapter on their own, even though neither of them had been able to read second-grade material independently.

Imagine what happened to their level of confidence and academic self-esteem! They began learning with vigor and endless enthusiasm. Thanks to TO/WITH/BY, caring teachers and Harry Potter, they could see the light at the end of the tunnel.

TO/WITH/BY is something that parents can easily do with their children at home. When a third grader, for example, is reading at a first-grade level and is unable to read Arnold Lobel's *Frog and Toad Are Friends* independently, then Frog and Toad books are the perfect homework! The student chooses a story from one of the books, his parent reads it TO him, then WITH him in unison, and then the parent supports him as it is read BY the student, who decides when to switch from TO to WITH to BY.

If you go into a California elementary school classroom in a large, urban school district during the language arts period, very often you will see every student reading the same grade-level story, whether they can handle that level of text or not. Some students are actually reading, but many of them are just mumbling along, pretending to read, hoping to get by. In many classrooms there is no instruction for struggling readers using books at their instructional level. When teachers are required by state or district mandate to teach reading with only grade-level passages, they might get better results by using the TO/WITH/BY strategy, being careful to provide strong voice support when the class is reading in unison. Of course, all the students who are unable to read the grade-level text would benefit from having additional instruction using appropriately leveled text. As the research shows us, struggling readers need instruction tailored to their needs every day (Allington, 2009a).

Independent Reading

Independent reading of books and other materials chosen by students supports and fosters reading comprehension and fluency, vocabulary development and writing proficiency, and the motivation to become literate (Krashen, 2004). The trick is to pair our struggling readers with books that are of interest to them and, at the same time, provide them with text that is accessible to them. This means that classrooms must be filled with hundreds of high-interest books at all levels of readability. When I walk into a fifth-grade classroom and see only novels, I am concerned. We create safe havens for reading when all teachers fill their classrooms with enjoyable paperback books (Krashen, 2011) at all levels and invite students to experience engaging characters like Frog and Toad and Harry Potter, along with graphic novels, comic books, joke books, and content area books about sharks and earthquakes. If we encourage all of our students to read exciting books at lower readability levels, then the struggling readers will feel comfortable reading books at their independent reading level. The more proficient students will soon get back to their novels and other more difficult text, and before long, our classrooms will resound with many more proficient, independent, happy readers.

When I taught a classroom of 34 second graders many years ago, they had a library period with another teacher. Each Wednesday right before lunch, my students would bring back a crate filled with the books they had checked out of the library that morning. After lunch they would crowd around me on the rug, excited to hear what I would say about their books. I would pull one of the books out of the crate and say, "Oh my gosh, who checked out *Mouse Soup*? This is one of my favorite books! Who has read this? Do you know the story about the bees? You don't? Okay, I have to read it to you—you're going to love this story!" Each time I raved about one of their books, the class was in awe of the student who had checked it out. I would overhear students asking each other if they could borrow their books after they were finished. I have come to believe that our greatest job as reading teachers is to let our students in on this secret: THERE'S NOTHING LIKE A GOOD BOOK!

In my experience observing thousands of youngsters read independently, it is true that children learn to read by reading (Smith, 1994), if they are reading extensively at their independent level. Struggling decoders who are participating in Rime Magic and SMILES instruction in their intervention groups need plenty of time to read independently every single day (Allington, 2009). When they reach a word-recognition grade equivalent of 4.0, and they have had a good running start with independent reading, they will take off like rockets as they read more and more books.

Read the beginnings of a variety of interesting books to your intervention group and ask them who would like to read the book you started. I read *Cirque du Freak* by Darren Shan to my group of sixth-grade RSP students in an urban middle school after they had completed the Rime Magic sequence and had made an average of two years' growth on their word recognition assessment. After about four chapters, they started trying to find the book in the school library to take home. Two of them talked their parents into buying all eleven books in the series over the next few months. You can imagine what happened to their fluency and their overall reading proficiency!

CHAPTER 10

Classroom Strategy Routines

Read, Read, Read!

If we want to support our struggling readers in our classrooms, the most important thing we can do is to have a classroom filled with exciting books at all reading levels, an area of the room dedicated to comfortable reading, and an expectation that all students will be engaged in reading every single day, at school and at home. Renowned reading researcher Richard Allington suggests that challenged readers should be spending as much as three to five hours every day reading at their independent and instructional levels—that's what it takes if we're serious about helping them catch up with their proficient peers (2009). In the context of this focus and the expectation that all of our students will be lifelong readers, we need to provide students with instruction that will do more than follow a teacher's manual written by people who have not met our students. Here are two classrooms that sparkle with effective and efficient reading instruction, followed by a Bay Area school district that is working hard to make a difference for all of its elementary students.

A First-Grade Classroom Model

In Kim Sugrue's first-grade classroom in San Lorenzo, California, you will see instruction that builds competence and confidence and a love of reading, and prevents children from moving up through the grades in need of remediation. While it is true that students come to us with a wide range of readiness for first-grade curriculum, a happy place full of leveled, predictable books and Magic Rimes provides a powerful start in closing that gap. Kim's students show more confidence and maturity each day as they gain strength with the strategies. You will even see her first graders teaching the Magic Rimes to each other! Here is a classroom that has integrated the Rime Magic strategies described in this book in such a way that first graders are ready to fly ahead in second grade. Below is Kim's testament to the power of these strategies.

It's been so easy to implement the Rime Magic strategies in my classroom! I had been teaching students to sound out words by looking at the first letter and sliding through each sound in a word. Once I saw the quick results of using Magic Rimes, I realized that my students could concentrate on developing their vocabulary and comprehension rather than spending so much time each morning sounding out words.

At the beginning of the school year I use the two-letter Magic Rime Cards with my whole class. When most of the class is able to recognize each rime in a longer word, I move the cards into student Learning Corners where they practice matching word cards with the rime in a pocket chart. My first graders also love to play "teacher/student" with the cards. In small groups of 3 or 4 students, they take turns "teaching" each other the rimes. Many of the students are able to practice the "finger spelling" with their small groups, too. After most students show proficiency with the two-letter rimes in a longer word, we move on to "the rest of the rimes" as a whole class and continue using the two-letter rimes in our guided reading groups for students who need more practice.

Another favorite strategy is a Rime Hunt in texts or passages. It is important for students to see the rimes in books, not just on flash cards. Last year, I was fortunate to have an interactive whiteboard in my classroom. I could project on the board a page from a familiar text onto the board and students could highlight rimes with their finger while the rest of the class highlighted a paper version at their table.

Long Vowel Spelling is an engaging way for my students to hear and see spelling patterns. It can easily be done on chart paper with the whole class sitting on the carpet using clipboards, or projected onto a screen with students writing at their desks. It's so great to see more and more of my class participating each time we do this activity!

I've been able to easily adapt every activity to fit the needs of my classroom. The magic of using these decoding activities will quickly become evident to teachers the moment a child looks at you bright-eyed and exclaims, "NOW I get it!"

—Kim Sugrue
First-Grade Teacher
San Lorenzo Unified School District

A Fourth-Grade Classroom Model

Now let's take a peek inside a fourth-grade classroom, also in San Lorenzo, where students are receiving instruction based on all the strategies included in this book as an integral part of a comprehensive research-based language arts curriculum. Cheryl Wozniak provides an excellent model for whole-class and small-group instruction, sharing her expertise with other teachers in her school district. Each year her class becomes efficient at working with her as a whole group on their comprehension and writing strategies, rotating through literacy-based centers, and meeting with her to receive small-group intensive, targeted instruction, Eventually they return to whole-class lessons for multisyllabic words and spelling. The magic occurs when all of the structures in her classroom fall within the context of a Book Flood! But I'll let her tell you about that.

Cheryl's class

The first year I switched from teaching middle school to teaching fourth grade, I learned that my fourth-grade students already had a wide range of reading abilities. Some students were reading on grade level, but many were not. Even though my students were given a lot of time in school for reading books of their choice, I realized what was holding them back, especially my English learners, was their lack of phonetic knowledge. When I was introduced to the Zinke strategies, I knew these strategies were what my students needed to fill the gap.

Students of all ability levels can practice the strategies and advance at an appropriate pace. For example, when doing Long Vowel Spelling, students select words that are accessible to them, so everyone feels successful. Let's say we are working on the long-*i* sound. I give students a minute to think of a word, and at the end of the minute I draw names for students to share their word. At first my students might share words such as *fly* or *my*. The *y* placed at the end of a word is one of the patterns that makes the long-*i* sound. After doing this activity a few times, my higher-performing students begin to stretch themselves and try to think of multisyllabic words, such as *environment*, that include the long-*i* sound, or words that have unusual spellings of the long-*i* sound, such as *Einstein*. Everyone is comfortable and enthusiastic during this activity!

The Zinke strategies are great additions to my literacy workstations (Diller, 2005). After we have practiced the strategies as a whole group, I include the activities as part of the word-study station or in a Zinke station of its own. During the language arts block, students rotate through literacy stations and work with a partner on a variety of reading skills. Workstation time is the perfect opportunity for me to instruct a small group of students who are still struggling with decoding. Using the Magic Rimes, I am able to help them make fast growth in word recognition while the rest of my class is reading independently or working on another literacy activity with a partner.

Ultimately, what matters to me is that the reading instruction that takes place in whole-group lessons, small groups, and literacy workstations supports my primary goal: to help students become proficient, lifelong readers. That is why all instruction is delivered in a room filled with books students love to read, and independent reading is at the core of my language arts program. Sharon's strategies have become an integral part of my literacy instruction because, with little time spent planning and preparing, they help me achieve this goal.

—Dr. Cheryl Wozniak
Fourth-Grade Teacher and Literacy Coach
San Lorenzo Unified School District

A District-Wide Model

The Berkeley Unified School District in California has made some wise choices over the years, keeping in place a strong structure for literacy support for the elementary schools. In addition, under the leadership of Head Literacy Coach Tom Prince, the district recently opted to bring in formal training from the Teachers College Reading and Writing Project, headed by Lucy Calkins at the Teachers College at Columbia University, providing support for elementary teachers in all of its elementary schools. Classrooms are filled with high-interest, leveled books and students spend a good portion of their language arts period reading, strategizing, and talking about books. Teachers supplement and enhance the decoding and spelling part of the literacy process with Magic Rimes and other strategies described in this book. Let's hear from Tom how the Berkeley elementary schools are folding these strategies into their exemplary literacy program.

When we started using Sharon Zinke's Magic Rimes with our students, we knew immediately that she had given us an invaluable new tool in helping develop more-accurate readers. Her system is deceptively simple, yet remarkably successful. Classroom teachers have added a few minutes of Magic Rimes to the beginning of their guided reading groups, and intervention teachers have made her program an integral part of intervention groups focused on accuracy. After just a few sessions, students start to understand "how words work" and demonstrate greater flexibility and success reading unknown words in isolation. Teachers can't help but be thrilled when they see that those same students are independently reading in text and are able to decode words quickly, efficiently, and accurately while reading. This allows these students to direct more of their attention to understanding what they are reading, which is the ultimate goal for all readers. It is rare that a single program such as Sharon Zinke's has had such a profound and effective impact on an entire school district's reading instruction.

—Tom Prince
Head Literacy Coach
Berkeley Unified School District

CHAPTER 11

What About English Language Learners?

English Language Learners are often negatively affected by an overemphasis on phonics and decoding instruction. They need English language and vocabulary development, and a quick, effective set of lessons to make sense of English letter-sound relationships and word structure. Most of the programs dominating California classrooms require too much time focusing on isolated phonics drills rather than lessons designed to help children make sense of the English language, with comprehension the goal. Kindergarten classrooms in some districts spend more than an hour each morning on scripted phonics instruction, with children squirming and finding ways to create art in the fibers of the rug on which they are seated. This phonics drill is often meaningless to these young children, especially English Language Learners, and a waste of precious instructional time.

Students learning English as a second language need to spend a great deal of time practicing oral communication in English. Heavy emphasis on phonics instruction often supplants critical oral language development. Students new to English need to build a foundation of oral English in order to benefit from structured practice in letter-sound correspondence.

Newcomers who are literate in their first language may be ready to jump right in and benefit immediately from Rime Magic instruction along with their oral language practice. They can transfer what they know about letter-sound correspondence from their first language to English. On the other hand, newcomers who are not literate in their own language benefit from lessons in oral language and vocabulary development and should not be spending significant amounts of time on English phonics instruction until their oral speaking and comprehension skills are developed. When these preliterate newcomers are ready to master English phonics, it needs to be done with the most engaging and efficient method possible.

We have found, in the urban school districts where there is a large percentage of students learning English as a second language, that when students have in fact developed their oral fluency and comprehension in English and are ready to take a closer look at the decoding of English words, the Rime Magic sequence is a fast and effective way to help them make sense of English word structure. It allows students to see initial onsets (consonants or consonant blends) and common word endings in the context of words that can be used in sentences that mean something to the students. They can see the rimes (word families, phonograms) jump out at them from inside words that make sense to them. A lesson can be as short as 10 minutes, but you will hear cries of protest if you try to stop that soon.

Students in bilingual programs benefit greatly from the Rime Magic sequence. They have an advantage over those who do not learn to read in their primary language. For example, with instruction in Magic Rimes, Spanish-speaking students easily make the transition from the Spanish alphabetic system, which breaks words into syllables, to the English system, which is more easily decoded by noticing the distinction in a syllable between onset and rime (Goswami & Bryant, 1990). Many phonics programs teach by dividing words into separate phonemes, which hinders comprehension and may slow the decoding process. Because the Rime Magic strategy makes use of letter "chunks" within words, it is generally easier for those English Language Learners who are transitioning from their native language literacy to English literacy

Some students have been designated as "Long Term English Learners," having attended ELD programs for five to seven years without fulfilling the requirements for redesignation to fluent English-proficient status. One of the things that holds these students back from being redesignated is their lack of competence in reading. Although reading proficiency is often delayed by a lack of vocabulary, academic language structures, and comprehension, a number of these students continue to struggle with decoding. They have spent years subjected to the same phonics programs that have not worked for them and have become creative in finding ways to tune out. These upper-elementary and middle-school students become quite enthusiastic when they are suddenly able to experience success during intervention with the Rime Magic sequence and lessons in decoding multisyllabic words.

This is equally true for students referred to as Standard English Learners (McWhorter, 2000)—those who speak African American dialect, for example, a full-blown, systematic, rule-governed language but not a mainstream dialect. Because the lessons are scaffolded, there is ongoing immersion without the possibility of failure, and lots of oral participation, these youngsters participate with energy and abandon. Young boys who were finding ways to distract themselves and those around them begin to sit up and pay attention, enjoying every minute of the lesson.

The Rime Magic sequence allows students to master English word structure in a very short period of time. English Language Learners and other students who enter school with limited vocabularies and little experience with books do not have time to participate in months and months of remedial lessons. They need a quick, effective intervention to rapidly catch them up to their peers in word recognition. This allows more time to be spent on vocabulary development, comprehension strategies, and the acquisition of academic English language structures. There is no reason to send our English learners to fourth grade reading at first- or second-grade level.

CHAPTER 12

The RTI Solution for Decoding

How do the strategies outlined in this book fulfill the instructional requirements of the Response to Intervention (RTI) model to meet the needs of struggling readers? Let's take a look, one tier at a time, and see how Magic Rimes and the rest of these effective decoding and spelling strategies can be used to keep students from falling behind in reading.

Tier I

Tier I intervention must be preventive and proactive (Allington, 2009a). Classroom teachers find all sorts of ways to help their students when they notice that they are struggling. In addition to finding ways to scaffold whole-class lessons to provide support for those who need it, they may pull a student aside for a quick review or reteaching of a particular concept. Or they might pull a small group together when they see that some of their students need reinforcement after a whole-class lesson. Many teachers organize all of their students into small, leveled groups and meet with them for instruction that is specific to the needs and capabilities of the group. All of this would be considered Tier I intervention. Skilled teachers are constantly monitoring their students as best they can to make sure everyone makes good progress.

Magic Rimes

When the Rime Magic sequence is folded into the language arts period in first grade and the beginning of second grade in a whole-class setting, you are taking the first step toward preventing future struggling decoders. Your Rime Magic lessons can be very short, from five to twenty minutes, leaving plenty of time for all of your other language arts instruction. This allows daily opportunities for focusing on comprehension with lots of independent reading time. Some of your first graders will make sense of the way words work right away, and some will benefit from consistent, ongoing lessons, immersing themselves in the rhythm and chanting of the rimes and spellings, becoming more proficient each day. Because the lessons are repeated again and again with pacing that keeps interest high, students who get stopped by other phonics lessons and begin to fall behind have a chance to develop an internal sense of the way words work. Short, daily Rime Magic lessons will go a long way toward making sure there are few if any struggling decoders in third grade.

Multisyllabic Word and Spelling Strategies

The immersion that supports and nurtures less proficient readers during Rime Magic lessons is also the guiding principal of the Base Word Constancy, SMILES, and Rime Word Spelling strategies. These whole-class strategies will challenge proficient readers and spellers and, at the same time, support students who struggle with spelling and decoding. Students who need more time to grasp the concepts governing English spellings are allowed the freedom to start by listening, and to participate more and more as they gain confidence and skill. Teachers who notice students who are not able to keep up with the written participation in the lessons can be pulled aside for extra practice in small groups.

Tier II

When a classroom teacher notices that a particular student or group of students needs a more consistent intervention and that their needs are not being met through Tier I classroom supports, he or she might work with other school personnel to plan a more structured small-group intervention. This might take place with a reading specialist or Learning Center teacher outside the classroom at a time that usually does not interfere with the students' core language arts instruction. Or, in some schools, a reading teacher might join the regular classroom teacher during the language arts period to provide small-group intervention. Some classroom teachers are able to set aside time for a small group of struggling readers several times a week, meeting their Tier II needs without outside support. Of course, the structure of Tier II intervention depends on the resources of the school and the district.

Magic Rimes

When students are reading below grade level because of decoding difficulties, small-group intervention using the Rime Magic sequence will provide fast results. Older students often require only a few lessons over a period of days or weeks before they have raised their word-recognition levels significantly. Students who are transitioning from reading instruction in their primary languages will find that the Rime Magic lessons help them quickly make sense of English decoding. The Rime Magic sequence is extremely helpful in identifying students with language-processing issues. When students have difficulty blending onsets with rimes or have letter-sequence confusion, the Magic Rimes will help them sort it out. They will make good progress with Rime Magic lessons accompanied by lots of shared, guided, and independent reading, but it will take longer for mastery to occur. Some of these students may require Tier III intervention.

Multisyllabic Word and Spelling Strategies

Although most students will make good progress with Base Word Constancy, SMILES, and Rime Word Spelling lessons in a whole-class setting, some will benefit from the comfort of doing these activities in an ongoing small group with other students who also need more time and support. This gives the classroom or support teacher a chance to closely monitor each student's spelling of the words, giving immediate feedback as needed.

Tier III

When a student has received Tier I and Tier II support and teachers find that sufficient progress is not being made, a plan must be created to give the student more intensive support. This might require one-on-one instruction by a teacher skilled in reading intervention for students with learning differences, or the student might even attend an alternative course of instruction that replaces the regular core curriculum, thereby getting more minutes per day of instruction aimed specifically toward his or her particular needs.

Magic Rimes

It has been my experience, having worked with struggling readers in special education settings for many years, that students who need intensive intervention in decoding will make much faster progress with the Magic Rimes than with traditional CVC instruction in phonics. Teachers who have used both approaches with students in Resource Specialist Programs (RSP) and Special Day Class (SDC) settings report with unbridled enthusiasm the tremendous growth they observe once the Magic Rimes are a regular part of the day. Students who need one-on-one tutoring will begin to smile and take pride in their progress, demanding the lessons each morning and even coming in at recess for more.

Multisyllabic Word and Spelling Strategies

The same is true with the Base Word Constancy, SMILES, and Rime Word Spelling strategies. Students in intensive Tier III groups will find success with these strategies when they realize that each step of their progress is honored and they can't really make a mistake that will cause any kind of shame. Mistakes are celebrated as important learning moments, and all of the struggle is taken out of the spelling of long words and words with long vowels. Of course, this success takes longer to transfer to spelling in their independent writing, but progress will be made and students will begin to have some strategies that will give them the confidence to stare a multisyllabic word in the eye as they read independently!

Intervention or Prevention?

What if we could prevent the need for intervention? At the very least, we must be committed to drastically cutting down on the number of students in our schools who need reading intervention. How would we do this?

I believe that the answer lies in our primary classrooms in the elementary schools. Instead of spending a large percentage of the morning in a first-grade classroom on phonics instruction driven by the teacher's manual of a basal reading program, let's fill our classrooms with interesting leveled books and have our students spend the greatest part of the morning reading at their independent reading level. Let's spend five minutes each morning with the Rime Magic sequence, leaving the rest of our language arts block for independent reading, small lessons in strategy instruction, or guided reading in small groups or with one student at a time.

Research tells us that phonics instruction is most effective if it is mostly completed by the end of first grade (Routman, 2003; National Reading Panel, 2000). If most of our students mastered the Rime Magic sequence in first grade, we could spend an amazing amount of time in the primary grades focused on strategies for comprehension, with lots of time for practice in the act of reading. Imagine the students a fourth-grade teacher would meet in September if instead of endless phonics lessons, they had been spending their primary-grade mornings consuming thousands of books, perfecting the art of metacognition and sophisticated comprehension practices, enjoying the incredible worlds to be found in books!

CHAPTER 13

Intervention That Makes a Difference

In California, our classrooms are bulging with a rich mix of students from all over the world, speaking many languages, bringing exciting cultural differences to the learning environment. Most often there is a vast range of language proficiency and readiness for school and learning in our kindergarten classes. Some of our new kindergartners come to school on the first day with full tummies and a rich literary repertoire, having listened to hundreds of books and participated in a wealth of rich conversations and literacy experiences. On the other hand, some arrive at kindergarten without the comforting nourishment of breakfast and have no idea what is inside a book or even how to hold it right side up. Many of these students have limited vocabularies and have never experienced a library or a story while cuddled on a soft lap. In addition, in some of our schools, English is a second language for more than half the class. Some of our new students are finding themselves in an English-speaking environment for the first time in their short lives. And finally, a few students in each classroom have differences in the way they learn, or have processing difficulties with print.

By the time these children reach second grade, some of them are considered "below grade level" in reading according to the latest content standards. Of course, when students fall behind their peers, there are many contributing factors, many of which are mentioned above. However, there are also system-based factors to consider. For the past 20 years, our government policymakers and state school boards have been mandating strict guidelines for teachers to follow when teaching language arts. In addition, legislation has been enacted that limits the programs and reading materials that teachers are allowed to use in their language arts instruction. Teachers are being asked to have all of their students read the same material, regardless of their reading ability. Students are being tested more and more often, taking valuable instructional time away from the school year. And most recently, class sizes are being raised because of budget constraints. These are only a few of the problems that affect the learning of students who desperately need an instructional program in which teachers are teaching to the specific needs of individual students.

The reality in most of our schools is that in each and every classroom there are students who are unable to read the material that is considered "grade level" for their grade in school. As we look at classrooms moving from kindergarten upward, the discrepancy grows wider and wider. In a fifth-grade classroom, we find several students who are reading two, three, and even four grade levels below their classmates. By the time they reach middle and high school, it begins to look hopeless for many of our students. They look for ways to avoid the daily frustrations and indignities of schools, teachers, classrooms, and books. We find them wandering the halls and hiding in class under the hoods of their sweatshirts. Students in fifth grade, middle school, and high school who are reading at first-, second-, and third-grade levels cannot afford to waste one more minute. They need reading intervention that works.

There Is a Solution!

Yes, there is a solution for students who have fallen far behind. When the National Reading Panel reached its conclusion that intensive phonics instruction is not effective for older, struggling readers (NRP, 2000), the authors had not found a phonics program that made enough of a difference for students who struggle with decoding. These students need an intervention that allows them to become proficient in decoding and word recognition within a few weeks or months, not years. Magic Rimes and the rest of the decoding strategies included here will make that difference, and fast.

The Rime Magic strategies are challenging to implement for students who struggle with word recognition in high school, somewhat less challenging in middle school, and EASY to implement in our elementary schools. The reason for this is related to school structure. In high school and middle school, there are very few structures in place where students who are far behind in reading can receive small-group or individual instruction. When a high school student is reading at first, second-, or third-grade level, he needs instruction that is designed to meet his particular needs. A full class using a commercial intervention program will not provide enough help fast enough. These students need to catch up immediately. This usually requires one-on-one and small-group instruction based not on moving through a program, but on the individual needs of the student. Yes, many of these students need phonics and word-recognition instruction as part of their intervention, but most programs repeat the skill lessons that did not work for these students in the first place. Often, the only resource for these students is within the special education department, and in high school even special education teachers do not systematically work with small groups or do just what the students need individually, opting instead to help them complete homework assignments and pass classes, leaving them just as far behind in reading proficiency as they were in the first place. However, when a middle- or high-school student is several years behind in reading, the strategies described in this book will bring him or her up to or near grade level in word recognition in a short time if the student can work one-on-one with a teacher or skilled volunteer (see Chapter 15, What About Middle and High School?).

The good news is . . . there is a very workable, efficient solution for students who are still in elementary school. When I go into an elementary school, the first thing I do is find out which students in each classroom have fallen behind in reading, beginning with second grade. This is usually determined by state or district test scores and teacher referrals. Students who score Below Basic (BB) and Far Below Basic (FBB) on the California Standards Test (CST) are given a quick word recognition assessment (I use the Slosson Oral Reading Test—S.O.R.T.—as I have found it to be highly reliable over the many years that I have administered it) to determine a word-recognition grade-equivalent score for each student. This grade-equivalent score, of course, is not a reading level, since comprehension is not taken into account. I use the test as a screening tool to find out who needs Rime Magic and other decoding remediation, and who does not (see Chapter 2 for the Rime Magic sequence). Second through sixth graders who have low word-recognition scores are given support in decoding, the amount and intensity of intervention depending upon the resources available in the school or district.

Students who score on or near grade level in word recognition are obviously not in need of remediation in decoding. These students, given that they scored very low on the state test or were referred by teachers as struggling with reading and writing, are given more intensive support in vocabulary development and reading comprehension, in addition to time for independent and guided reading. With high or grade-level scores in word recognition, we can assume that vocabulary or comprehension challenges likely account for their reading difficulties.

Students who score under 3.0 in word recognition in the upper grades are placed in groups according to their word-recognition grade equivalent. Students who score between 2.0 and 3.0 are grouped together. Those who score below 2.0 can be grouped together even if some score below 1.0. The students who have the lowest word-recognition scores (.1 to .5) will become immersed in the Rime Magic chanting and spellings, following along with the others, becoming more proficient each day. However, if students scoring above 2.0 are grouped with lower-scoring students, it is very likely that they will provide spellings too quickly and drown out the others. All of these students are given Rime Magic instruction by their classroom teacher during the language arts block or by literacy support staff if the school is fortunate enough to have a literacy coach, reading intervention teacher, or special education staff who can work with small groups.

Students who score between 3.1 and 4.0 are given a quick set of Rime Magic lessons (two times through the sequence), and then move on right away to lessons in structural analysis, including Base Word Constancy and SMILES. These activities can also be easily implemented in the regular classroom as whole-class lessons, with a sharp eye out to make sure that these particular students are able to keep up with the lesson.

A couple of years ago I was asked to work with a group of nine fifth-grade students in an urban elementary school who had fallen behind in reading. Their word-recognition grade equivalents ranged from .8 to 2.9. After only five to seven 20-minute lessons, mostly with one to three students in a group, six of the nine students had made between 1.5 and 3 years' growth. Two more made between .6 and 1 year's growth. One student did not attend school on the day of the final assessment.

One fourth-grade boy was spending quite a bit of his day out in the hall because he was disturbing his class. His teacher said that he was angry and noncompliant and, since the beginning of the year, had refused to participate in reading instruction. Day after day he would watch my little group of students out in the hallway, inching closer each time. Finally, I asked if he would like to join us and he began to sit with us every day, fully engaged in all of our activities.

After-School Reading Intervention

There are many models for after-school reading intervention that will make a difference if efficient, targeted instruction is at its core. Tutors from local colleges and volunteers can be utilized, as well as teachers who choose to provide instruction after school is out for the day.

One inner-city elementary school in California has adopted an after-school intervention model that has proven successful in raising the word recognition scores of students who have fallen behind. Of course, it would be best if we could afford to hire after-school teachers to provide this intervention, allowing classroom teachers to spend their hours after class preparing for the next day. However, due to funding limits, eight classroom teachers met twice a week for 45 minutes right after school with four to six of their own students who scored significantly below grade level in word recognition.

The intervention took place during six weeks in the spring with first, second, and third grade students. The 45-minute session was divided into two sections: Decoding and Comprehension. First graders received Rime Magic, Shared and Partner Reading, and TO WITH BY, in addition to a retelling activity to improve vocabulary and comprehension. Second and third graders received an additional lesson in multisyllabic words (SMILES). Because of time constraints, teachers received only one afternoon of staff development and then two or three sessions of side-by-side coaching while they were with their intervention students after school. Even though teachers had minimal training in teaching the strategies and had not yet used them in class during the year, they achieved significant results. The struggling readers received between 10 and 12 sessions with their classroom teacher. Out of 36 students who were served, nine students made between one and five months' growth (this group contained seven students receiving special education services), 17 students made between six months and a year's growth, and 10 students made between one and two years' growth in word recognition.

The teachers who participated in the after-school intervention were excited about the growth that their students made in such a short time. They were looking forward to folding the strategies into their classroom instructional program the following year.

Intervention Structures for Fast Progress

Based on the word-recognition levels of students being targeted for intervention, we have found that particular structures are most effective in bringing decoding ability up quickly so that the struggle is removed from the decoding or the recognition of words on a page.

For students who score below .3 on the Slosson Oral Reading Test, identifying fewer than ten words in isolation from the word lists, the Magic Rimes are appropriate for English-speaking students who are in first grade or above. These students benefit from the TO/WITH/BY strategy (see Chapter 9) and lots of shared reading of connected text found in simple poems, in Big Books, in predictable trade books such as *Rain* by Peter Spiers, *Go Dog Go* by P. D. Eastman, *The Very Hungry Caterpillar* by Eric Carle, and in predictable books such as *Mrs. Wishy Washy* by Joy Cowley. These students need fun lessons in interactive writing or in an individual or group language experience story. They need to build up reading strategies in their guided reading groups. Ideally, each classroom has access to sets of leveled books that can be used for guided and independent reading. These students also need a chance to write every day, using what they know about letter-sound relationships to spell the words in their stories as best they can. They need to be read to every day, talking with each other and with the teacher about exciting stories and interesting content area material. Linda Hoyt's *Interactive Read-Alouds* (2006) is an excellent resource for making the most of reading aloud to your students. It is critical that these students have a span of time each day to read familiar predictable books or books that have been matched to each student's reading level, independently or with a partner, practicing the strategies that they have learned, building up fluency and confidence.

For students who score between .3 and 1.9, all of the above activities are appropriate and highly effective. We begin to raise the level of the predictable books for shared reading and the TO/WITH/BY strategy to books such as the Frog and Toad series, *Owl at Home*, or *Mouse Soup* by Arnold Lobel, and of course, *Green Eggs and Ham* by Dr. Seuss. It is important that they have lots and lots of shared reading and writing, independent reading and writing, and that they are read to every day. These students are capable at this stage of actively participating in the entire sequence of Rime Magic strategies and the reinforcement activities that accompany them. *Note*: When grouping these students for work with the Magic Rimes, it is best to separate those who score between .3 and .9 from those who score between 1.0 and 1.9. This will give students a better chance of fully participating in the lessons. However, at this level, if they are grouped together, the less proficient decoders will chime in with the others and before long, they will develop mastery through short, daily repetitions of the Rime Magic steps.

For students who score between 2.0 and 3.0, all of the shared, guided, and independent reading and writing activities and read-alouds continue to be important. Again, the level of books chosen for independent and shared reading will rise for these students. Frog and Toad will quickly become easy enough to read independently, and more sophisticated books can be used for shared reading. One of my favorites is *Fables*, another wonderful book by Arnold Lobel, and students at this level will enjoy all of the wonderful books by Robert Munsch. In addition, you might bring in books that students are interested in reading that are at a frustration level. After using the TO/WITH/BY strategy chapter by chapter or paragraph by paragraph, your students will be very excited to be able to read what was out of reach before, and their confidence will climb to new heights. Students at this word-recognition level, given consistent attendance, will move fairly rapidly through the Rime Magic sequence, and will be able to participate right away in the multisyllabic word and spelling instruction. Since the multisyllabic word and spelling strategies can easily be taught in whole-class lessons, struggling readers at this level can be closely monitored during whole-class lessons in upper-grade classrooms and/or given extra instruction in a small group.

Progress through the Rime Magic sequence at this level is very fast for students without processing difficulties that qualify them for special education services. Special education students who have language processing issues will still make progress, but it will take more repetitions of the strategies and more time spent reading independently and with support.

Two Fabulous Summer School Models

What if summer school actually worked for reading intervention? Here are two models that have shown that this is both possible and fairly easy to accomplish. Before we created our first one last summer in San Lorenzo, California, I had not held out much hope that summer school could do much to change a student's prospects for the future. As far as I could tell, summer school was "more of the same." Some schools do pre- and post-testing that takes up much of the precious instructional time, without seeing significant results. Often, in middle and high school, it is just a chance for students to get credits that had not been earned during the school year. More and more, inner-city schools have stopped providing classes for enrichment and offer summer school only to students who are struggling with reading, writing, and math. If students are going to spend a good part of their summer break trying to catch up with their peers, we had better offer them a summer intervention program that makes a difference!

Summer School in a Week

This was a big surprise! When the administrator of an inner-city elementary school in Richmond, California, informed me that we only had one week to provide summer intervention for our lowest-functioning readers (because the regular district summer school would begin a week after school was out), I was ready at first to give up on the idea. However, whenever I asked the students if they would come for three hours in the mornings during the week immediately following school dismissal for the summer, I got a resounding positive response. So, we went for it!

Six classroom teachers volunteered to teach an intervention group of six students each. We invited the 47 students at the school between grades two and five who had the lowest word recognition scores and we were surprised to get parent permission from 40 families. Exactly 36 students showed up the first morning, having no idea of what to expect. One thing the students were probably not expecting was to be in small groups of six the entire time, where they would get the full attention of the teacher and had no place to hide!

The summer school teachers received five hours of staff development designed by myself and Angela Barra, ELD (English Language Development) consultant for the district, in very specific strategies that would be implemented in each group. These strategies included the Magic Rime sequence for all students, the multisyllabic word strategy (SMILES) for all except the group that had scored below 1.0 on the word recognition test, and time spent on comprehension, fluency, writing, and Independent Reading in appropriately leveled books.

The results of this summer experiment were more than encouraging. Many of the upper-grade students had been flying through text with very little comprehension due to regular DIBELS fluency testing where they had been asked to read as fast as they could, timed with a stopwatch, without being asked to retell, discuss, or answer questions about their reading. These students improved in their ability to retell sections of text after a week of lessons focusing on vocabulary and comprehension. This result is anecdotal, because with only a week of instruction, we were unable to gather objective data on improvement in comprehension.

However, in the area of word recognition, students had baseline scores from the Slosson Oral Reading Test that had been given at year's end, and, since it is a quick assessment, we decided to assess again on the fifth morning of summer school. Our students were demonstrating such enthusiasm and showing so much improvement even on the third and fourth day that we decided it was worth taking a look. Out of 36 students, after only four mornings of targeted instruction, more than half made over five months growth in word recognition, and even more astounding, three of our students made between one and two years growth, and one fourth-grade girl made over two years growth!

There were other significant indications of success. The teachers who participated in this program, having experienced disillusionment and frustration during the regular school year with budget cuts and mandatory fidelity to programs that they could see were not making a difference for their struggling readers, began to lighten up over the course of the week. Teachers who were in the habit of leaving meetings the instant their time was up found themselves sitting far past the ending time in our daily debriefing meetings at the end of each morning. They had so much to share about the successes of their six students! We often had to remind them that our meeting had gone over and they could leave for the day. In addition, teachers began sharing, sometimes tearfully, how they could now see changes they wanted to make for the upcoming school year. After years of resisting the implementation of small-group instruction in their classrooms, they began to talk about how they would set up small groups to meet the needs of their struggling readers. They brainstormed ways to blend the strategies that they had learned during the summer into their school day so that they could prevent students from moving to the next grade reading far below grade level. They began to feel the excitement that brought them to teaching in the first place!

Summer School in a Month

Teachers at Lorenzo Manor Elementary School, inspired by the sudden word recognition growth of students receiving instruction in Magic Rimes and SMILES during the year, decided to launch a custom summer school for one month in the weeks before the next school year began. Four classroom teachers were recruited to work with 20 students each, along with one reading intervention instructor. One teacher had students entering first and second grades, one had students entering second and third grades, another had students entering third and fourth, and one, fourth and fifth. Students were placed in these four classrooms with their word recognition scores as well as grade level in mind. School officials decided to keep it local, inviting only the students at Lorenzo Manor who were having the most trouble learning to read and had the lowest test scores on state, district, and teacher-created assessments.

Summer school opened in late July, which gave teachers and students several weeks to relax after the school year had ended and to prepare an exciting schedule to support their superheroes theme. The daily schedule included all the strategies included in this book, along with comprehension strategies, some math instruction, and an amazing Book Flood. Cheryl Wozniak, fourth-grade teacher at Lorenzo Manor Elementary School, served as reading intervention specialist and lead teacher. Read what she reported about the month-long Superhero Summer Reading Program below.

Lorenzo Manor Summer School

I have taught summer school in the past, but never before have I been part of a summer program where both teachers and students were this happy to be at school during their summer vacation. I attribute that to three key factors: an exciting theme that tied the learning activities together, a flood of Superhero books and other graphic novels, comics, and books of high interest to students, and the Zinke strategies. The combination of these three made for an unforgettable summer learning experience!

Superhero Theme

For the past two years I had been adding many superhero graphic novels and comics to my classroom library, and I saw what a positive difference this made in my students' reading attitudes. Suddenly, students who had not had an interest in reading before were excited to read and couldn't wait to check out another comic book. So I proposed that we capitalize on this enthusiasm by utilizing the superhero concept in our summer school program. And it worked! Students of all grade levels were excited about the theme and couldn't wait to read more superhero books during summer school.

Book Flood

Central to the success of the summer school reading program was the Book Flood. My principal approved a budget of four thousand dollars for books, so I purchased a few hundred books, many of which were graphic novels, for students to read at home and in school. Dressed as Wonder Woman, I visited classrooms and conducted weekly book talks and read-alouds (Wozniak, 2010). Students could hardly contain themselves when Wonder

(continued)

Woman delivered the new books each week; they read insatiably. One teacher tracked the number of books her students read, and by the end of the four weeks her students had read close to 300 books!

Zinke Strategies

Sharon Zinke's strategies were the foundation for both the classroom reading instruction and the small-group intervention. For example, in the two upper-grade classrooms, the following Zinke strategies were part of the daily instructional schedule: Magic Rimes, Long Word Strategies (Base Word Constancy and SMILES), and Long Vowel Spelling. Comprehension strategies and TO WITH BY were implemented every other day. As the reading intervention teacher, I worked in all four classrooms. I pulled small groups of students and taught all of the Magic Rime activities. The daily repetition of the Zinke strategies not only were beneficial for students but also made it easy for the classroom teachers and me to plan.

All three of the components of the Superhero Summer Reading Program worked. Students were receptive to the theme, loved reading the books, and were engaged during the Zinke strategy lessons. Best of all, our daily attendance was at an all-time high! Few students dropped out or were absent, and students were excited and willing to talk about their summer school experience when they returned to school only one week after summer school had ended. Too often students as well as teachers simply go through the motions of summer school but never gain much. Students enrolled in Lorenzo Manor's Superhero Summer School Reading Program not only improved their reading skills and became better readers that summer, they also left loving to read! For me, that was the real success.

Cheryl Wozniak
Reading Intervention Teacher
Lorenzo Manor School

CHAPTER 14

Students With Learning Disabilities *CAN* Learn to Decode

When I pass by the open doors of Learning Centers or other classrooms in which students who receive special-education services are working, students will often try to get me to come in and "do the rimes" with them. They love the Magic Rimes because they can see right away that it's working!

Students who have qualified for a Resource Specialist Program (RSP) or who attend a Special Day Class (SDC) are very often struggling with reading and writing and usually have a word-recognition level that is far below grade level. Researchers are finding that special-education students who enter special education two or more years behind in reading do not catch up with their peers and can be expected to fall farther behind (Allington, 2009a; Denton, Vaughn, & Fletcher, 2003). Many of the students who have qualified for special education services have language-processing issues that cause significant letter confusion. The letters appear to them in confusing visual sequences or arrays that do not allow them to "sound out words" in the same way as their peers. For example, the *p* at the end of *slap* may appear to the student to be right after the initial s, so that the students reads *slap* as *spal* or *spattle*. Most of the usual remediation techniques used in special-education settings to address the needs of these students do not bring the desired results quickly enough, and often make no difference at all (Allington, 2009a). Because many special education teachers believe that these struggling students will never achieve much growth in decoding, students are taught to "compensate" for their disability as best they can. While it is true that some struggling students with a Specific Learning Disability (SLD) can learn ways to compensate for their decoding difficulties, many just fall farther and farther behind, finally finding themselves sitting in the back rows of high school classrooms, hoping no one will notice them, pretending to have forgotten their glasses, dreaming of dropping out.

Resource Specialists, Special Day Class teachers, and Learning Center teachers are very excited and encouraged when they are introduced to the Rime Magic sequence of lessons. When they observe their struggling readers respond so quickly and with great enthusiasm to the Rime Magic lessons, they can see right away that fast progress will be made and that many of their students have a good chance of successfully joining their peers in content-area instruction. When the students themselves are exposed to the Rime Magic sequence, they can see almost from the first five minutes that it will make the critical difference for them. They begin to sit up and pay attention.

Resource Specialists, Special Day Class teachers, and Learning Center teachers are very excited and encouraged when they are introduced to the Rime Magic sequence of lessons. When they observe their struggling readers respond so quickly and happily to the Rime Magic lessons, they can see right away that fast progress will be made and that many of their students have a good chance of successfully joining their peers in content-area instruction.

The Learning Center Model

The Learning Center model that is becoming more popular in the Bay Area of California brings students with Individual Educational Plans (IEP) together with other students who are struggling with learning to receive intervention during the school day in small groups outside the regular classroom. This is an ideal situation for remediation in decoding because students can be grouped initially according to word-recognition level. We group them this way for decoding instruction so that each student is able to process and problem-solve without interruption by a more capable student. After students with decoding issues are given some time with the Magic Rimes, they can participate more fully in the ongoing comprehension instruction in the Learning Center and in their regular classrooms. Because the Rime Magic decoding intervention takes so little time, the largest block of intervention time can focus on strengthening comprehension.

Embedded Rime Bonus Cards

Students who have language processing difficulties that affect fluent reading and who have qualified for special education services often have great difficulty blending word parts and may perceive the letters in words in a somewhat scrambled sequence. These struggling decoders benefit greatly from reinforcement in the form of Embedded Rime Bonus Cards.

For example, one set might be based on the rime *at*. The words might include *flat, splatter, scratching, splat, matches, scattered,* and *flatten*, among others.

These bonus cards are usually not necessary for students who have no letter confusion, although any student who has fallen two or more years behind in word recognition will improve very quickly with the supplemental use of Embedded Rime Bonus Cards. Those students who have a mild to severe text-processing challenge will benefit greatly from one-on-one supplemental instruction using the Embedded Rime Bonus Cards. Because the rime remains constant while the onset and endings change, they are able to work on blending the rime within the word in such a way that they will learn to straighten out their own letter confusion. When the student needs any assistance at all with a word, the word goes to the back of the pile and comes up again later. For example a student might add the letter *r* to a two-letter blend at the beginning of a word (*scramper/scamper*) and have a difficult time removing the *r* from the word even after it is pointed out to him. Or he might add the letter *t* (*stettered/settled*) or the letter *l* (*plubish/publisher*) to the single consonant at the beginning of a word. While it is true that this same student might decode the word *publisher* correctly in the context of connected text, this shifting of letters slows the student down considerably and is a daily frustration. By allowing these struggling decoders plenty of time to attempt the word each time it comes up in the stack of bonus cards, we enable them to take control of the process and find success on their own. Each time the student sees the card, it becomes easier to do the blending. He is teaching his own brain what it needs to know. This is highly motivating to struggling readers who have spent years feeling helpless.

My upper-elementary RSP (Resource Specialist Program) students were determined to get through all of the Bonus Cards as quickly as possible. Almost every day at recess there was a banging on my classroom door and a request to "do the Bonus Cards." Struggling readers who had spent the past three to five years mystified by the sequence of letters in words were training their own brains to "get those letters to behave!" When the *at* in *scratching* jumped out at them, that pesky onset (*scr*) began to settle down and stop moving around.

The Embedded Rime Bonus Card Set contains a set of words for each of the 35 Magic Rimes and 30 of The Rest of the Rimes. The Bonus Card Set is not included in the DVD and can be purchased separately at www.rimemagic.com. Full instructions are included.

CHAPTER 15

What About Middle and High School?

My motivation for writing this book comes from what I have seen in classrooms where adolescents have emerged from their elementary schools unprepared for what awaits them in middle and high school. Teachers in middle and high school for the most part do not expect to teach reading. They are excited about the content in their particular instructional areas and look forward to sharing their expertise with students who have the nuts and bolts of reading solidly under their belts. Many are surprised to find students in their classrooms who are unable to read the assigned material, depend on other students to get them through classroom activities, bring back little or no homework, disappear from class at opportune times, finding any way they can to get through another day at school. These teachers are often unprepared for the complications of having such a range of reading proficiency in their classrooms, and as much as they would like to help their students, are not sure how to do it this late in the game.

Middle schools and high schools are scrambling to accommodate the high numbers of students who show up in September reading far below grade level. Some schools create special reading or literacy classes for students who are struggling in the language arts. This adds tremendous complications to already complex scheduling. Do students in middle school, for example, miss out on their history/language arts block to have a remedial class in reading and writing? Do remedial classes in high school earn credits? Will they make enough progress to attend regular English classes? These questions have no easy answers.

Middle- and high-school students who are reading far below grade level need very specific instruction and access to books that are of high interest and at their independent reading level. Obviously, they will not get this kind of instruction in most regular English classes. If they are far enough below grade level to require Rime Magic instruction (below 3.0 or even 3.5 on a word-recognition test), they will need to work one-on-one or in a small group with a reading teacher or tutor. This instruction could be done with a larger group if the students were all at similar word-recognition levels. However, most remedial classes showcase a range of reading difficulties. Some students are much stronger in word recognition—and may even be decoding on grade level—while grappling with vocabulary or comprehension issues. Rather than remediation in decoding, they need a significant amount of time reading and discussing books, with demonstrations of and practice in metacognition. Good comprehension instruction benefits all students regardless of their decoding proficiency and lends itself to whole-class instruction. It is the students whose word-recognition grade equivalents are at first-, second-, and third-grade levels who need to work with others at a similar level in a small group.

A Middle-School Story

Before I retired from 40 years of teaching in California's public schools, I took a position as a Resource Specialist at a middle school. My caseload of 24 sixth graders included 12 students who were reading far below grade-level expectations. Although they were bright, inquisitive youngsters, their word-recognition grade-equivalent scores ranged from .9 to 2.8. Because their ability to recognize or decode words was so far below grade level, they had very little access to the printed assignments in their English, history, science, and math classes. Some of these middle-school students had fairly strong listening vocabularies, but their lack of word attack skills prevented them from making sense of grade-level text. There were so many words they could not recognize or "sound out" that they could not comprehend their textbooks, assigned literature, or even their homework assignments. When I observed in their classrooms, I often found my RSP students with hoods on, heads on the desk, attempting to grab the attention of nearby students, sneaking text messages, or doing careful wheelies inside their desks with tiny skateboards. Most often, sitting in class meant passing time until the bell saved them from a wrenching boredom.

This was unacceptable to me as a former reading specialist. Undaunted, I began to experiment. My extensive experience as an elementary-school resource specialist had taught me that instruction based upon onset/rime was a much superior way to present letter/sound correspondence to any student, but especially those with "learning disabilities" that affect decoding and encoding proficiency. Having observed dozens of popular phonics programs pass through California classrooms for several decades, it made perfect sense to me that children recognize and blend word parts together more easily when they are perceiving larger chunks rather than attempting to distinguish every separate phoneme.

Working with my 12 sixth-grade students, I soon developed a set of strategies that brought about fast and efficient progress in decoding and word recognition. Although we were impeded by constant scheduling issues and had to spend a significant amount of time on math, writing, study skills, and keeping content-area grades from slipping, after our work with Rime Magic and the other strategies described in this book, 10 of my 12 students ended the year with grade-level word-recognition scores. The other two students made two and three years' growth. Now these 12 students could access their grade-level texts enough to participate in general-ed classroom activities along with their peers. Classroom lessons in vocabulary development, enhancement of prior knowledge, and other reading- and writing-related comprehension activities did not fly over their heads. Their attention improved dramatically, they were able to follow along with reading assignments, and most of all, several of these personable and inquisitive students realized for the first time in many years that they were not "stupid" and could participate fully in an academic group activity.

A High-School Story

On an overcast summer morning I sat waiting for Tyrell, a hard-hitting varsity tight end in an urban high school. Looking around the small, cluttered special-education office, I wasn't sure if he would show up for another meeting with another teacher, another meeting that was not his idea. I was ready with all my favorite assessment tools, prepared for any possibility. Sadly, I had been told by a special education administrator that he was probably "borderline developmentally delayed" and would never make significant progress in reading. The district's special education department had requested that I spend 20 remediation sessions with Tyrell to see what I could do. I chose to see Tyrell as I see all children who struggle in school—a boy who had, for some reason, not been served adequately by his school system, a boy who was capable of anything and everything.

Tyrell peeked around the door, leaned his red custom-built bicycle against the wall, and kept his eyes lowered as he sat down opposite me. I could barely hear his voice. After attempting some small talk, I decided to plunge in. "Has anyone told you what this meeting is about?" I asked. He shrugged. I thanked him for coming to see me and asked him about his success on the football field. After a while I began to acknowledge his experience of years and years of feeling like a failure with no one really able to help him with his reading, program after program that didn't work, teacher after teacher who wasn't able to help him catch up with his friends. During this conversation he began to look up to see who he was talking with. When I had his attention, I let him know that I was absolutely certain that together we could raise his reading level. I could tell that he had decided to trust me a little, at least for a few minutes.

Tyrell's assessment results showed us that we had a challenge. Based on the QRI IV, Tyrell was reading at second-grade level. His word-recognition grade equivalent was 2.1, yet his behavior during passage retelling led me to believe that his comprehension was much stronger and that we could raise his reading level when we had dealt with the decoding and word-recognition issues. He shyly admitted that he never ever reads because "it's too hard." I asked him what he wished he could read. He wanted to be able to read his mechanics manual for a class he was taking at City College, but it was far out of reach. He agreed to bring it to our session the next day. Tyrell looked at me like I was dreaming, but my confidence was infectious, and he agreed to show up the next day at the same time.

It was about fifteen minutes into Tyrell's second session when he began to perk up and look alive. He could see that this might just work. He began to sit up straight and make eye contact, his voice displaying a new presence and determination. I knew we would win this game.

After 20 45-minute sessions, Tyrell had made remarkable improvement. His word-recognition grade equivalent score had risen two and one-half years, to 4.6. He was able to decode words like "combustible" and "transmission" in his car mechanics manual and showed determination and commitment as he made his way through the text, although he had not had time yet to develop fluency. His IRI assessment showed that he was able to do a strong retelling of passage after leveled passage. When we had successfully completed the seventh-grade passage, he announced that he didn't want to do any more, even the next day. He was done. I heard nothing from the family until one day toward the end of the school year. Tyrell's mother was on the phone, sobbing, thanking me for what I had done for her son. I was finally able to understand that she was telling me that Tyrell had passed the language arts section of his high school exit exam.

Yes, Tyrell was a student who had fallen through the cracks. His special education teachers were stunned at his fast progress. It is to students like Tyrell that I dedicate this book.

CHAPTER 16

But Wait! Where Does the Magic Come From?

Why do these strategies work so well to bring the word-recognition levels of struggling readers up to grade level? When I first developed the Rime Magic sequence, I was surprised by how quickly my students broke free from the hold that their decoding difficulties had on them. I have asked myself what makes Rime Magic more effective than other approaches that have only chipped away at the problem.

Access to the Middle of the Word

Providing developing readers with a way to clearly see the rime within a word, beginning with words that consistently act the same way, allows them to march forward with renewed confidence. Instead of relying only on the beginning letter(s) of a word to help with constructing meaning as they read, students who in the past had perceived an unruly string of letters are now able to see those letters as a series of familiar "chunks." Readers who have struggled for years are able to see right away that this is different from other phonics lessons and that it's going to work. And teachers who have spent so many hours of planning and teaching time trying to find ways to help the students in their classrooms who seem to make so little progress are stunned to see their struggling readers jump ahead so easily.

Early Success

Struggling readers of any age need to see that what we are asking them to do is going to make a difference. Middle and high school students who have spent year after year in remedial reading groups and classes, given program after program with the same phonics lessons, brighten up and pay attention when they see right away that the Magic Rimes are the key to unlocking many of the words that have stumped them in the past. Because students are taught to recognize the Magic Rimes within words that are consistently short-vowel, multisyllabic words, they are able to develop a strong foundation right away. In their very first Rime Magic lesson, students are able to locate the rime in a two- or three-syllable word and easily decode the word. Eyes light up immediately and hope turns to confidence before the end of one lesson. Engagement is everything: when students feel successful and competent, they enjoy learning. The most important path to motivation for struggling readers is early success (Routman, 2003; Allington, 2001).

Respect and Autonomy

Effective teachers have always known that what makes the biggest difference in their classrooms is shared respect. When I walk into a classroom where students are thriving and everyone seems happily engaged in learning, I see a teacher who is valuing each student for the contribution he or she makes to the classroom community. When I talk with my struggling readers, they can see my confidence in their success right away. I look into their eyes and talk straight to them about their strengths and gifts. As they meet with me each day, they feel stronger and more responsible for their own success. The most important gift we can give our reading intervention students is confidence and a feeling of success (Stipek, 2002). When students feel respected and honored for who they are, they begin to feel accountable and willing to take responsibility for their learning. Giving students choices leads to feelings of autonomy. Within the parameters of the goals we set as intervention teachers, we can give students choices of topic, tasks, and time. When students feel successful and have some power over the process, fast progress is possible.

Positive Reinforcement

What's the difference between stickers and genuine acknowledgment? In my experience, there is an ocean of difference! Extrinsic motivation in the form of prizes or pizza might be motivating at the moment, but it causes excitement about the prize. We want our students to be excited about *reading*. We want them to be excited about books and their new ability to get lost in a story or to learn about absolutely anything! Our struggling readers need to hear thousands of positive statements about their attempts at literacy. When I think about how many negative experiences a high-school boy reading at second-grade level has had over the past ten years or so, I am deeply saddened. How many F's has he seen on his spelling tests and other assignments? How many times has he been told that if he would just pay attention, he would learn something? How many of his teachers have given up on him in frustration? How much disappointment has he seen reflected on his parents' faces?

How can we make up for all of this negative input? Each struggling reader needs to hear positive acknowledgment of his unique gifts and of each tiny step in his progress during every reading-intervention session. Even better, what if each small improvement were encouraged and acknowledged all day long in each of his classes?

I keep all of this in mind as I work with struggling readers. I tell them every last thing that I notice about how smart they are, how right they are, and how I knew they could do it. Every moment in an intervention group is an opportunity to cancel out one of the thousands of negative comments that make up the way many of our struggling readers see themselves.

Trust

Most commercial programs are structured into what publishers and authors consider a sequence that will move students comfortably through carefully thought-out levels of instruction. The problem with most programs is that everyone is often expected to move at the same pace. Some districts require teachers to conform to the schedule of a pacing guide, even if many students have not achieved success along the way. We need to observe our students to see what they need, with the understanding that each child is different, learns at a difference pace, and has unique gifts and challenges. And we need to trust teachers to know their students and to make decisions based on what those students need rather than what a pacing guide or a teachers' manual indicates is the next step for the class. And then we need to trust our students to learn! Students are always learning. Sometimes they are learning that school is boring, that reading time is frustrating, or that they are deficient in some way. What if they were able to participate in lessons that are scaffolded and motivating and meet their particular needs, while being surrounded by books at their independent reading level so they can practice what they have just learned?

No Frustration

All of the strategies outlined in this book are designed to allow students to learn in a stress-free environment. First of all, intervention students who need decoding instruction are grouped with others who function at nearly the same accuracy level in their reading and have similar problems recognizing words or blending parts of words. During Rime Magic lessons the group chanting allows students to chime in with others who are somewhat more proficient without requiring students to perform solo. The Rime Magic activities and the whole-class instruction in multisyllabic words and spelling are highly scaffolded and leave very little room for frustration. Struggling readers begin to stop struggling and relax into the lessons, feeling more confident each time.

Wait Time

Teachers who observe my intervention groups often comment on my level of patience. I believe that this patience comes from my certainty that every student is capable of more than he or she knows, and of much more than has been expected in the past. Often, because of time constraints, we feel pressure to press forward, attempting to move as quickly as possible through a planned lesson. But there is a huge payoff in allowing the time for students to process what seems simple to us but may be a new and challenging abstraction for our students. Teaching a concept isn't enough. It needs to be processed and discovered and digested and practiced by the learner, and that often means that we have to include "wait time" in our interactions with our students.

Eye Contact

Many students who struggle with reading have mastered the art of "hiding out" in their classrooms in order to avoid embarrassment. They will sit across from you at your intervention table and pretend to participate as they do every day in class. As soon as you look down at your Magic Cards, they will find something else of interest in the room. For this reason, it is especially important to engage your students with eye contact. I do not start any part of the Rime Magic sequence of activities until I have confirmed eye contact with each student in my group. I do this gently and with a sense of humor. Very soon, their sharp focus on the activity at hand becomes a habit.

Immersion Before Mastery

Struggling Readers who have had difficulty with decoding and encoding need plenty of time to process what is offered to them in the Rime Magic, multisyllabic-word, and spelling strategies outlined in this book. It is important that we do not expect mastery at every juncture. In each part of the process is a whole array of opportunities for students to develop proficiency at their own pace. You will find that some students are very quiet at first, maybe even just watching. Understandably, children or adults learning a new language often do this, just observing and not trying to speak out loud for a period of time. Learning to see the parts of words is a similar challenge for some of our students. As they are immersed in the rimes and the lessons continue day after day, they will begin chiming in with the more confident students. As they watch the words being placed in boxes on the Long Vowel Spelling chart, attempting to fill in the words on their own papers, they will begin to feel confident enough to raise their hands to contribute. If struggling readers are allowed the comfort of continued immersion without pressure, mastery will be the result. And of course, mastery of the act of reading comes as a result of hours and hours of independent reading for pleasure. We must not forget our intended result!

Scaffolding

Closely related to immersion, scaffolding is a critical element in the success of struggling readers. When students are asked to spell the word *shimmering*, they are able to see the colorful rime (*im*) surrounded by your fingers as placeholders for the letters of the onset (*sh*), the extra *m*, and the two endings (*er* and *ing*). All of this scaffolding, along with the blended voices of the teacher and the rest of the students in the group, provides so much support that it is hard to make a mistake. And if a student does say an incorrect letter, your response is positive!

> If a student spells *s-t* instead of *s-h* at the beginning of the word *shimmering*, I respond, "You're right, it starts with an *s* . . . now listen . . . *shhhimmering*. Do you hear the *shhhh*?" The student will either self-correct and say *s-h*, or not. If he does not know the *sh* digraph, I just tell him casually that *s-h* spells *sh*, and we go right on, respelling the word, with the understanding that there will be many more opportunities to learn the digraph.

The Base Word Constancy and SMILES lessons are similarly scaffolded. Students can follow along with you, separating affixes and the rest of the syllables, always with immediate feedback, until they begin to see the separate word parts as they come across a multisyllabic word in their reading and hear the separate syllables as they are spelling a particularly long word as they write. Everyone learning something new and challenging needs a certain amount of scaffolding. I only need to imagine myself learning to work on a sputtering car engine to be perfectly clear about this.

Pacing

All of the lessons described in this book need to move forward at a fairly good clip. Does this sound contrary to the concept of giving students plenty of time? Because the lessons are so scaffolded and you are giving students time to think, your students will find it easy to move briskly through the lesson and will be more likely to remain fully engaged. Avoid the temptation to teach at every "teachable moment." If you do, you run the risk of losing the rapt attention of all of your students. This is especially important when your students are volunteering words during Long Vowel Spelling. It's important to keep the pace going rather than stopping to discuss spelling rules with the class. They will become familiar with spelling patterns as you repeat the lessons each week. Your pace will improve as you become more familiar with the teaching processes and you benefit from practice over time.

The Magic Rime Cards are the most challenging at first for most teachers. It can feel awkward at first to place your fingers quickly and smoothly in front of and behind the Magic Rimes. However, as you get more practice, you will become more and more comfortable holding the Magic Rime Cards and your fingers in place at the same time.

Brisk pacing is especially important during decoding lessons since decoding is a small part of the reading process. We want to slow down and give most of our thoughtful attention to strategy instruction, comprehension activities, and plenty of time for independent reading. We need to keep our decoding lessons short and focused, with an eye toward slowing down at just the moments that will support our struggling readers. Who said good teaching isn't a challenge?

Play

When students are reading significantly below grade level, it's serious business. We must immediately do something about it, and we must show students that the intervention time is important. However, I have had the best results over the years when I keep my interactions with the students in my intervention groups somewhat light and playful. Smiles and laughter here and there are like adding a little spice to a fine meal. Lessons are livened up, the affective filter is down, and there is room for concern to diminish and for struggle to disappear. Humor is a universally recognized way to relieve stress—and stress has darkened the academic lives of some of our struggling readers for years. Having fun with our students is the best medicine. It's always a good idea to create an atmosphere in which a good book is associated with positive feelings, happiness, and smiles.

Middle School Ready

My dream is to send every student to middle school reading on or close to grade level, ready to participate fully in classroom literacy activities with his or her peers. After what I have seen in the past several years as I have worked with teachers in elementary schools all over the San Francisco Bay Area, I know that this is possible. While it is true that we have students who need time to learn English as a second language, there should be only around 2 percent (Allington, 2009) of our students who have learning challenges that require so much extra time that they might leave elementary school significantly behind their peers in reading. That means that we should be able to close the gap for 98 percent of our elementary students who fall behind their peers in the early grades. If we provide our elementary students with instruction that engages them at their level of need and inspires them to move ahead feeling good about every step of their progress, if we have the tools and insights that will make the difference, we can send our elementary students into their new middle-school classrooms prepared for the challenges ahead. It is my promise to the world that all children will learn to read with ease and with dignity.

Bibliography

Allington, R. (2001). *What really matters for struggling readers: Designing research-based programs.* New York: Addison-Wesley Longman.

Allington, R. (2009a). *What really matters in response to intervention.* Boston: Pearson Education, Inc.

Allington, R. (2009b). *What really matters in fluency: Research-based practices across the curriculum.* Boston: Pearson Education, Inc.

Bear, D. R., Invernizzi, M., Templeton, S. & Johnston, F. (2000). *Words their way: Word study for phonics, vocabulary, and spelling instruction.* Upper Saddle River, NJ: Merrill (an imprint of Prentice Hall).

Calkins, L. (2001). *The art of teaching reading.* New York: Addison-Wesley Longman.

Carle, E. (1981). *The very hungry caterpillar.* New York: Philomel Books.

Clymer, T. (1963). *The utility of phonics generalizations in the primary grades.* Originally published in RT (Vol. 16)

Cowley, J. (1980). *Mrs. Wishy Washy.* Auckland, New Zealand: Shortland Publications Limited.

Cunningham, P. (2008). *Words for reading and writing.* Boston: Pearson Education, Inc.

Cunningham, P. (2008). *What really matters in vocabulary: Research-based practices across the curriculum.* Boston: Pearson Education, Inc.

Cunningham, P. (2012). *What really matters in spelling: Research-based strategies and activities.* Boston: Pearson Education, Inc.

Cunningham, P. & Hall, D. (1998). *Month by month phonics for upper grades: Systematic, multilevel instruction for upper grades.* Greensboro, NC: Carson-Delosa Publishing Co.

Denton, C. A., Vaughn, S., & Fletcher, J. (2003). Bringing research-based practice in reading intervention to scale. *Learning Disabilities Research and Practice, 18*(3), 201-211.

Developmental Reading Assessment®, Second Edition (DRA™2) © (2005) Professional Development. Boston: Pearson.

Diller, D. (2005). *Literacy work stations: Making centers work.* Portland, ME: Stenhouse Publishers.

Eastman, P. D. (1961). *Go Dog Go.* New York: Random House, Inc.

Fearn, L. & Farnan, N. (2000). *Interactions: Teaching Writing and the Language Arts.* Boston: Houghton Mifflin Company.

Geisel, T. (Dr. Seuss) (1960). *Green eggs and ham.* New York: Random House, Inc.

Goodman, K. (2006). *The truth about DIBELS: What it is, what it does.* Portsmouth, NH: Heinemann.

Goswami, U. & Bryant, P. (1990). *Phonological skills and learning to read: Essays in developmental psychology.* Hillside, NJ: Earlbaum.

Hoyt, L. (2006). *Interactive read-alouds: Linking standards, fluency, and comprehension.* Dublin, Ireland: FirstHand Publishing.

Kalen, R. (1978). *Rain.* New York: Greenwillow Books.

Krashen, S. (2004). *The power of reading: Insights from the research.* Portsmouth, NH: Heinemann.

Krashen, S. (2011). *Free voluntary reading.* Santa Barbara, CA: Libraries Unlimited.

Leslie, L. & Caldwell, J. (2010). *Qualitative Reading Inventory,* 5th edition. Boston: Allyn & Bacon, Inc.

Lobel, A. (1970). *Frog and Toad are friends.* New York: HarperCollins Publishers, Inc.

Lobel, A. (1977). *Mouse soup.* New York: HarperCollins Publishers, Inc.

Lobel, A. (1980). *Fables.* New York: HarperCollins Publishers, Inc.

Lobel, A. (1982). *Owl at Home.* New York: HarperCollins Publishers, Inc.

McCracken, R. & M. (1996). *Spelling through phonics,* 2nd edition. Winnipeg, Manitoba: Peguis Publishers.

McWhorter, J. (2000). *Losing the race: Self-sabotage in Black America.* New York: Harper Perennial.

Miller, D. (2002). *Reading with meaning: Teaching comprehension in primary grades.* Portland, ME: Stenhouse Publishers.

Moustafa, M. (1997). *Beyond traditional phonics.* Portsmouth, NH: Heinemann.

National Reading Panel. *Report of the National Reading Panel: Teaching children to read.* (2000). Washington, D.C. U.S. Department of Health and Human Services.

Routman, R. (2003). *Reading essentials: The specifics you need to teach reading well.* Portsmouth, NH: Heinemann.

Shan, D. (2000). *Cirque du Freak.* New York: Little, Brown and Company.

Slosson, R. (1978). *Slosson oral reading test: A brief measure of reading ability.* New York: Slosson Educational Partners.

Smith, F. (1994). *Understanding reading: A psycholinguistic analysis of reading and learning to read,* 5th edition. New York: Routledge Publishers.

Spier, P. (1997). *Peter Spier's rain.* New York: Yearling Books.

Stipek, D. (2002). *Motivation to learn: Integrating theory and practice.* Boston: Allyn & Bacon, Inc.

Tatum, A. (2005). *Teaching reading to black adolescent males: Closing the achievement gap.* Portland, ME: Stenhouse Publishers.

Van Manen, M. (1986). *The tone of teaching.* Portsmouth, NH: Heinemann.

Wozniak, C. L. (2011). Reading and talking about books: A critical foundation for intervention. *Voices from the Middle,* 19, 17-21.

Wylie, R. E., & Durrell, D. D. (1970). Teaching vowels through phonograms. *Elementary English, 47,* 787-791.